ALL-NEW,
ALL-NATURAL
APPROACH TO BEATING
DIABETES

ALL-NEW, ALL-NATURAL APPROACH TO BEATING
DIABETES

Pat Harper, R.D., and Richard Laliberte
with William A. Petit Jr., M.D.

The Reader's Digest Association (Canada) Ltd.
Montreal • Singapore

CANADIAN PROJECT STAFF

EDITOR
Pamela Johnson

DESIGNER
Andrée Payette

COPY EDITOR
Gilles Humbert

READER'S DIGEST ASSOCIATION (CANADA) LTD.

VICE PRESIDENT BOOK EDITORIAL
Robert Goyette

HOME & HEALTH PROJECT STAFF

EDITOR
Marianne Wait

DESIGNER
Rich Kershner

CONSULTANTS
William A. Petit Jr., M.D.
Associate Professor of Clinical Medicine, University of Connecticut School of Medicine; Medical Director, Joslin Diabetes Center affiliate at New Britain General Hospital

Nancy Wright, Certified Personal Fitness Trainer

READER'S DIGEST HEALTH PUBLISHING

EDITOR IN CHIEF AND PUBLISHING DIRECTOR
Neil Wertheimer

MANAGING EDITOR
Suzanne G. Beason

ART DIRECTOR
Michele Laseau

READER'S DIGEST ASSOCIATION, INC.

PRESIDENT, NORTH AMERICA GLOBAL EDITOR-IN-CHIEF
Eric W. Schrier

Library and Archives Canada Cataloguing in Publication

Harper, Pat
    All-new, all-natural approach to beating diabetes / Pat Harper and Richard Laliberte with William A. Petit, Jr.

Includes index.
ISBN 0-88850-791-7

    1. Non-insulin-dependent diabetes--Popular works.
I. Laliberte, Richard II. Petit, William A III. Title.

RC662.18.H37 2006	616.4'620654	C2005-905702-5

Address any comments about
All-New, All-Natural Approach to Beating Diabetes to:
The Reader's Digest Association (Canada) Ltd.
Editorial Department
1100 René-Lévesque Blvd. West
Montreal, QC H3B 5H5

To order copies of
All-New, All-Natural Approach to Beating Diabetes,
call 1-800-465-0780.

Visit our websites at www.rd.ca or www.rdasia.com

Printed in China

06 07 08 / 5 4 3

Note to Readers
The information in this book should not be substituted for, or used to alter, medical therapy without your doctor's advice. For a specific health problem, consult your physician for guidance.

Credits
FOOD PHOTOGRAPHY: Sang An, David Bishop, Beatriz daCosta, and Elizabeth Watt
EXERCISE PHOTOGRAPHY: Cara Howe/StudioW26
FIRST PERSON PROFILES: Jason Cohn
COVER PHOTOS: Photodisc (1), © David Bishop (2), Photodisc (3), © David Bishop (4)

Acknowledgments

I would first like to thank the Diabetes Obesity Intervention Trial team at the University of Pittsburgh: David Kelley, M.D., principal investigator, for his vision, guidance, and support; Cindy Kern, R.N., project coordinator, for her organizational skills, professionalism, and impeccable attention to detail; and Juliet Mancino, M.S., R.D., for her extraordinary counseling skills and expertise as a diabetes educator. I am also grateful to Judy Arch, R.D., and Anne Mathews, M.S., R.D., for their assistance with this study and their contributions to other weight-loss studies in the division of endocrinology.

I would also like to thank some others who helped me with this book: Nancy Wright, exercise expert and owner of The Wright Fit, for her creativity and expertise in structuring the physical activity recommendations, and Charlene Rainey, of Food-Nutrition Research, Inc., for her invaluable insights. A special thank you to my coauthor, Rich Laliberte, whose persistence, patience, and talent for writing made the book a reality.

I would especially like to thank the people who volunteered for the DO IT study. Their determination to lose weight by changing their diets, increasing activity, and adopting healthier lifestyles was an inspiration to me.

—Pat Harper, R.D., M.S.

Creating this book was a team effort, and my hat is off to my terrific partners, coauthor Pat Harper and editor Marianne Wait. Pat is the kind of person you want in your corner when facing a disease like type 2 diabetes. Her warmth, experience, and research skills enable her to get dramatic results without ever forgetting the appeal of a chocolate chip cookie. I'll miss talking with her about the recipes in these pages, when I could almost hear her salivate as she'd say, "It's really good."

Marianne kept us on track with her incisive thinking and persistent drive to keep our advice consistent, clear, and fresh. Her dedication and high standards made this project the best it could be, and her guidance, comments, and laughter are the unsung, invisible heart of the book. I'd also like to thank our medical advisor, William Petit, M.D., for clarifying critical questions and ensuring that our plan is safe.

My biggest thanks go to my wife, Rachelle, and our children, Jordan and Marissa, who tolerated several months of deadlines with good humor and were even inspired, like me, to think more critically about what goes down in the family kitchen.

—Richard Laliberte

contents

Introduction

SMALL STEPS, BIG RESULTS

As publisher of the world's most widely read magazine as well as one of the world's top publishers of health books, Reader's Digest felt compelled a few years back to address the biggest health threat facing North Americans today: obesity. So we put together a team of top doctors, nutritionists, and health writers and developed a weight-loss plan that we believed was the most sensible, most effective, and safest around.

The result was the extraordinary *ChangeOne* program, which helped hundreds of thousands of people lose weight simply, safely, and, we hope, forever. Its premise is straight-forward: Making one small change at a time is the best way to bring about big results. Rather than trying to flip a switch and change all your eating, exercise, and stress-management habits at once—as so many diet programs ask you to do—with *ChangeOne,* you learn a single new skill, practice it until it's a habit, and only then move on to the next. Participants love it as well as its underlying message—that these changes are easy, healthy, and will last for the rest of their lives.

Right away, we realized that the same message applies to other important health goals, so it was only logical that we tackle another scourge plaguing our nation: the diabetes epidemic. More than 2 million Canadians have been diagnosed with diabetes, and by the end of this decade, the number is expected to rise to 3 million.

Unlike many other chronic diseases, type 2 diabetes is a condition that's strongly influenced by diet and lifestyle. In fact, the more research we did in preparing to develop this book, the clearer it became that people could bring down their blood sugar levels by changing what they ate and how much they moved their bodies.

In one of the most impressive studies we looked at, con-ducted at the University of Pittsburgh School of Medicine, type 2 diabetes patients dropped their fasting blood sugar levels by an average of 25 percent just by following a simple plan to help them lose weight. There was no structured diet, no carbohydrate counting, no specific fat or carbohydrate goals, no banned foods. The idea was to adopt a lifestyle, not to go on a "diet."

The approach in the study was so effective—and so in line with the *ChangeOne* philosophy—that we based *All-New, All-Natural Approach to Beating Diabetes* on it.

With this book, you'll lose as much as 10 percent of your body weight on the 10 Percent Plan. You won't do it by cutting out entire food groups or depriving yourself of snacks or desserts. Instead, you'll follow the Plate Approach, a visual guide to eating that cuts calories but still lets you enjoy your food. There's no math involved. What's more, all foods are fair game, although you may need to eat some of them in smaller amounts or prepare them a little differently. (We've even repaired 18 popular "disaster foods" for you.)

Because exercise is so important, you'll also follow the Forward by Five Walking Plan, which asks you to add just 5 minutes a week to the amount of time you walk each day. And you'll use feel-good stress-reduction techniques and other lifestyle approaches (such as getting more sleep and even having a massage) to lower your blood sugar naturally.

All-New, All-Natural Approach to Beating Diabetes is a solution you can stick with for life. That simple fact puts it well ahead of trendy low-carb diets, which many people have an extremely hard time staying on because they're too restrictive. And it's effective—so effective, in fact, that it could help you use less diabetes medication or even get off medication altogether.

Better still, the steps you'll take on the 10 Percent Plan actually help your body become less resistant to insulin—in effect, reversing your diabetes (although nothing can *cure* it). Best of all, they can help stave off complications such as heart attack, nerve pain, kidney disease, and serious eye problems, including blindness.

If you can change one small habit today, then another tomorrow, you can beat diabetes. So start with Step One of this plan and consider it your first step toward a healthier, happier, more energetic future.

Neil Wertheimer
Editor in Chief
Reader's Digest Health Books

nat

ural

(nat•u•ral) a*djective*

1. Being in accordance with or
determined by nature.

2. Not acquired: INNATE.

3. Without drugs. That's what *we* mean
when we use the word. And believe it
or not, it is possible to control your
blood sugar naturally.

PART ONE

The Natural Solution

introducing
THE 10 percent plan

You've opened this book for one simple reason: You (or a loved one) have diabetes or pre-diabetes, and you want to get it under control. Maybe you'd like to reduce your reliance on medication. Maybe you're hoping to avoid the day when drugs become necessary. Maybe you just want to know that you're doing everything in your power to keep your blood sugar in line and keep dangerous health problems at bay.

No matter what your situation, if you have type 2 diabetes, *All-New, All-Natural Approach to Beating Diabetes* will help you tame it.

Here you'll discover a remarkably effective approach we call the 10 Percent Plan. Follow it, and you could lower your blood sugar by an impressive 25 percent.

You'll also boost your cells' ability to respond to insulin. And you'll do it all with a completely safe, proven plan that will benefit your body from head to toe. Are you ready to take back your health?

A New Approach to Blood Sugar Control

If you have type 2 diabetes, your primary goal is simple: to bring your blood sugar under control. There's just no better way to protect your body from the ravages of the disease. By doing so, you'll help stave off diabetes-related complications, such as serious eye and kidney problems; reduce your risk of heart disease (did you know that people with diabetes have two to four times the usual risk of heart disease and stroke?); and most likely live longer. Best of all, you'll feel more in control of your day-to-day health.

How to bring blood sugar down is another matter entirely, and one that can seem anything but simple. Medications are one way, of course, and you may need to be on some. But there's more you can do to control your disease and slow its progression, starting with what you eat. There are a million different ways (at least, it seems like a million) to regulate your diet, from counting carbohydrate grams in food (in order to balance your carb intake throughout the day) and tabulating food exchanges to choosing foods according to their glycemic index ratings. We don't think you should need to do research on a food before you eat it, though, or carry around a notebook to keep track of everything you put in your mouth.

This book presents a different idea—a simpler approach. We think getting control of diabetes doesn't have to be all that complicated. In fact, it shouldn't be, because the more complicated a piece of advice is, the less likely you are to follow it. Approaches that involve a lot of time, attention, and planning can be difficult to keep up with permanently.

The truth is that all you really need to do to make a radical change in your health is to make small changes in some of your everyday habits, such as what you eat for lunch or what you do during TV commercials. How can small changes possibly add up to controlling diabetes? Keep reading, and we'll explain.

Bonus Benefits

Defeating diabetes by lowering your blood sugar is reason enough to lose weight. But stepping lighter on the scale may also help relieve or prevent a multitude of secondary health problems, including:

> High blood pressure
> Heart disease
> Stroke
> Gallbladder disease
> Joint pain
> Sleep apnea
> Arthritis
> Breast cancer
> Colon cancer
> Prostate cancer
> Kidney cancer

A WEIGHTY PROBLEM

Most people with type 2 diabetes have one thing in common: They weigh too much. In fact, nearly 90 percent of people with this form of diabetes are overweight.

That's no coincidence. Being overweight is the single most important contributor to its development—and losing weight is the single most important step in getting it under control (or preventing it).

What does weight have to do with diabetes?

Think of excess body fat as a contaminant in your fuel system. Glucose, or blood sugar, is the fuel that powers your body. Normally, glucose, which you get from the food you eat, has no problem making its way into your cells from the bloodstream. But body fat mucks up the process. It does its devilish work by releasing substances called free fatty acids into the blood.

Free fatty acids have at least two undesirable effects. One is to cause cells to ignore the glucose and leave it floating in your blood, which is what diabetes is all about. The other is to cause your pancreas to produce less insulin, a hormone that cells need in order to absorb glucose. Taken together, these effects make free fatty acids bad news—and not just because they play a major role in diabetes. The havoc they wreak on glucose absorption and insulin production also contributes to high cholesterol, high blood pressure, elevated triglycerides (another type of blood fat), and other problems that lead to heart disease.

Losing weight is like cleansing your fuel system so you use energy more efficiently. The less body fat you have, the fewer fatty acids you will have circulating in your bloodstream, and the lower your blood sugar will be.

The 10 Percent Plan

So how much weight do you need to lose in order to significantly bring down your blood sugar? Perhaps 18 kg (40 lb)? Maybe more? The answer is 10 percent of what you weigh now. Less than you thought, right? Consider how little 10 percent is. Ten percent of an hour is just 6 minutes. Ten percent of a pizza is barely a slice. And if you currently weigh 90 kg (200 lb), 10 percent is just 9 kg (20 lb).

Diabetes Dictionary

Here are some terms you need to know.

Type 2 diabetes. The most common form of diabetes, accounting for about 95 percent of all cases. The basic problem is that the body's cells can't soak up enough glucose, so glucose stays in the blood. In addition, the pancreas may not produce enough insulin, and the insulin may not work properly. This can cause serious complications throughout the body, including heart disease; high blood pressure; and kidney, eye, and nerve damage. Once called adult-onset diabetes, type 2 is becoming increasingly common in children, probably because kids are becoming more and more overweight.

Glucose. The body's main source of energy. Glucose, also known as blood sugar, originates in plants and is passed up the food chain. When it accumulates in the blood, it makes blood stickier. This makes it harder for blood to flow, which deprives the body of oxygen and nutrients, hinders white blood cells in fighting infection, and makes dangerous blood clots more likely. Glucose also attaches to proteins all over the body and affects their function.

Insulin. A hormone produced in the pancreas that acts like a key, "unlocking" cells so that glucose can enter. In type 2 diabetes, the pancreas can't keep up with the body's demand for insulin.

Insulin resistance. A condition in which cells become less responsive to insulin. Boosting cells' sensitivity to insulin overcomes this resistance so insulin has a greater effect.

Fasting blood glucose (FBG). The amount of glucose in your blood after not eating or drinking anything for at least eight hours before the test. A blood glucose of 7.0 mmol/L or greater indicates diabetes.

HbA1c or hemoglobin A1c—also known as glycosylated hemoglobin. A test that measures your average blood sugar level over the previous several months. It measures how much glucose has become attached to the protein hemoglobin, an oxygen-carrying component of red blood cells. A score higher than 9 means you need more control, below 7 is acceptable, but less than 6, which is normal and ideal, is desirable.

A 10 percent weight loss and the corresponding drop in blood sugar will make you feel better almost immediately—by getting rid of the jittery feelings that blood sugar swings can cause and giving you more energy, for example. Over the long haul, it will also substantially cut your risk of diabetes-related health problems, such as poor circulation and kidney damage. Just as important, losing 10 percent of body weight typically brings down cholesterol levels, blood pressure, and overall risk of heart disease.

Why 10 percent? First, because it's relatively easy to achieve. (Most university- and hospital-based weight-loss programs produce a 10 percent weight loss in six months.) More important, though, it's an amount that's virtually guaranteed to lower your blood sugar.

We know that losing 10 percent has a huge impact because we've seen it work in studies—not just in overweight people but also specifically in people with type 2 diabetes. One recent study took place at the University of Pittsburgh School of Medicine. The goal of the participants was to achieve and maintain a weight loss of at least 7 percent. What made this study different from others was its approach, particularly regarding eating. *There was no structured diet.* No carbohydrate counting, no food exchanges, no specific fat or carbohydrate goals, no banned foods. The idea was to adopt a lifestyle, not start (and therefore potentially stop) a "diet."

After six months, the participants had actually overshot their weight-loss targets, losing an average of 10 percent of their body weight, and the resulting drops in blood sugar were even more impressive. The study worked so well that we based our 10 Percent Plan on it.

REMARKABLE RESULTS

Participants in the study, officially called the Diabetes Obesity Intervention Trial (DO IT), were given basic dietary guidelines to follow, and then they made their own choices about what to eat. Each week, a dietitian offered suggestions on how to make the meals and snacks they were eating slightly healthier. The idea was to improve the people's current eating habits here and there, a little at a time, instead of trying to get them to adopt a whole new way of eating. In this book, we'll help you carry out just such a plan yourself.

The other key component of the study was physical activity. Here, too, the goal was not to start an exercise "program" per se but to work more activity into people's everyday routines, starting with small amounts of walking and gradually building more steps into each day.

For six months, the participants went about their normal lives while applying the principles of the plan. Then they went to the clinic for an extensive series of tests and evaluations that required an overnight stay—something they'd done at the start of the study as well. One of those tests isn't available at your doctor's office but is used by researchers: It's a test for insulin sensitivity, which indicates how well cells are able to use insulin. After another six months, the people went back to the lab again.

The results were nothing short of spectacular. By sticking to simple guidelines, the study participants:

- Exceeded the 7 percent weight-loss goal, losing an average of 10 percent of body weight after six months.

- Kept weight off through the end of the year-long study. Although average weight bounced back slightly, on average, the participants were still more than 8 percent below their starting weights after a year.

- Reduced their fasting blood glucose from dangerously elevated levels into nondiabetes territory. (Test results reported in U.S. measurements were reduced from an average of 170 mg/dL [9.4 mmol/L] to 125 mg/dL [6.9 mmol/L]—a 45-point difference.) An average drop of more than 25 percent.

- Brought their hemoglobin A1C levels (a measure of glucose averages over a period of three months) down from an average of 8 (typical for people with diabetes) to 6.7, which

Can You Get Off Your Meds?

For many people on the 10 Percent Plan, one of the biggest payoffs will be getting off medication or insulin or taking less. We can't make promises: You need to make treatment decisions with your doctor, especially when it comes to any changes in medication. But here's what you might expect if you succeed in bringing your blood sugar down to the following levels:

- **7 to 7.8 or 8.3 mmol/L:** While still above normal, these levels are low enough that you may be able to stop taking all medication.
- **8.3 to 11 mmol/L:** The chances are good that continuing to follow the plan may allow you to get off medication. For now, however, you may still need medication and perhaps occasional doses of insulin.
- **Above 11 mmol/L:** You may need medication or full-time insulin coverage, and possibly both, but the plan may let you reduce your doses or make other adjustments. What's more, it will most likely lower your blood pressure and improve your cholesterol numbers. And of course, you'll enjoy a greater sense of control over your health.

is just above the desirable level of 6 recommended by the Canadian Diabetes Association.

- Improved their insulin sensitivity by fivefold in some cases and, in many cases, by twofold. Because the sophisticated lab tests for insulin sensitivity aren't accessible to the average person, you won't be able to measure your own improvement in insulin sensitivity, but if you have better glucose control with less medication, you can be sure your sensitivity has improved.

- Were able to stop taking medication. This was true for 18 of 25 people who were taking drugs at the start of the study.

- Matched the weight loss of a control group that followed the plan and also took the weight-loss drug orlistat (Xenical). Think of it: By using entirely natural methods, people in this study achieved the same results as peers who tried to get a boost from a weight-loss drug. That's powerful medicine.

Not everyone can expect these exact results, of course. For research purposes, none of the participants weighed more than 136 kg (300 lb) (lab measurement equipment couldn't handle people that heavy). To make sure researchers could tell which results came from lifestyle changes, none of the partici-pants was on insulin. Those who were on medication needed to be able to quit their regimens for the study and safely maintain an acceptable blood glucose level. Regardless of these factors, though, anyone with type 2 diabetes can significantly benefit from the approach used in the study.

As if the results of the DO IT study aren't impressive enough, there's even *more* you can do to bring blood sugar down naturally and reduce your risk of diabetes-related health problems—and you'll do it on the 10 Percent Plan. These measures won't necessarily help you lose weight, but they will give you extra leverage when it comes to lowering your blood sugar. They include:

- Relaxation techniques that help improve your glucose con-trol by reducing levels of "stress hormones" that raise blood sugar

- Improving sleep patterns and battling sleep deprivation, which has been linked to increased insulin resistance

Taking the Plan on the Road

Vince Petroy was ready for a change. At 180 cm (5'11"), the 58-year-old sales manager tipped the scales at 108 kg (239 lb) and had blood sugar levels ranging from 13 to 15 mmol/L. "My goal was to stay off medication," he says. "I saw my parents taking scads of pills, and I just didn't want to be like that."

What struck him about the approach of the DO IT study—which is also the approach of the 10 Percent Plan—was how easy it is. "It's very simple, and I followed the guidelines exactly," he says. "All it really takes is deciding you want to be healthy." Even though he spends most of his time traveling with members of his sales team, he found ways to stick to the plan. In some ways, it even made life easier. "I'd get jittery when my blood sugar was uneven," he says. "And if I was running for a plane, I'd just grab a candy bar, which made things worse. It turned out that the best way to control my swings was to make sure I took time throughout the day to eat better foods." For breakfast, he favored cereals such as Raisin Bran. Lunch might be a turkey sandwich with a bowl of broth-based soup. He kept dinners light and early. And for snacks, he'd have an apple, an orange, some raisins, or a handful of nuts.

The biggest challenge was exercise. "Initially, it wasn't easy to make myself get out to do the walking," Petroy says. "But once I got into the rhythm, I'd feel out of sync if I didn't do it." While on the road, he'd go for a walk as soon as he checked into his hotel. In the morning, he'd get up early and hop on a treadmill in the hotel gym. "By the end, I was walking an hour a day almost every day of the week," he says.

His results astonished him. It was as if he were on a miracle drug—but without the drug. After a year, he maintained a weight loss of 12.2 kg (27 lb) (well over 10 percent of his starting weight) and had dropped his average blood glucose readings to around 6 mmol/L. "My sugars were absolutely normal," Petroy says. But that was only the beginning. He also found he was brimming with energy and slept soundly, without tossing and turning. "Guys I travel with used to joke, 'Has Vince had his nap yet?'" They were amazed at my energy once the weight came off. I just feel great. It's been a total win for me."

- Simple strength-training exercises that build muscle and boost your metabolism so you'll burn more calories

By incorporating all the elements of the DO IT study plus these extra components, the 10 Percent Plan can deliver even more impressive results, making your chances of dropping your blood sugar by 25 percent all the greater.

WHY THE PLAN WORKS

Lots of weight-loss plans (and programs for diabetes) offer good ideas about what *should* work. What makes the 10 Percent Plan so effective? Surveys of participants in the DO IT study and others point to a number of factors that contribute to the plan's power to succeed.

- It corrects a number of simple but fundamental errors committed by many people trying to lose weight, such as going too long without eating or saving the biggest meal for the end of the day. It also ensures that you cover all your basic nutritional needs without ever feeling hungry.

- It never restricts what you can eat, although you may need to eat favorite foods in smaller portions or prepare them in different ways. A typical sentiment from DO IT participants: "It didn't feel like a diet."

- It's a plan you can live with. Although recent research has tentatively bolstered weight-loss claims made for popular low-carb diets—at least in the short term—doctors and dietitians find that many people have an extremely tough time staying on these diets for the long haul because they're too restrictive. The 10 Percent Plan can produce significant results that become a regular way of life, not just a temporary fix.

Another important reason to follow this plan is that it's been proven to work for people with type 2 diabetes. The eating schedule in the 10 Percent Plan is specifically designed to keep blood sugar levels from swinging wildly between highs and lows as well as to ensure that you eat fewer calories so you lose weight. Unlike many low-carb diets, the plan is careful to steer you clear of dangerous fats that make blood sugar control more difficult and raise your risk of heart disease—already a big danger if you have diabetes—and focus on the ones that actually facilitate better blood sugar control. You'll be eating unlimited amounts of vegetables, so you'll get plenty of the nutrients that people with diabetes need most (not to mention plenty of food, so you won't be hungry). And the exercise you'll get on the plan will help to increase your insulin sensitivity and further decrease your blood sugar levels.

Because the plan doesn't involve math, it's easy to follow. There's no calorie or carbohydrate counting (except for an initial one-time assessment of your current diet), you don't have to try to make sense of the confusing glycemic index, and we won't ask you to eat your burger without a bun or pass up potatoes. You're allowed to eat bread and pasta, and even dessert, in reasonable amounts. Yes, you will need to make some changes—for instance, eat a little less fat, fill your plate with more vegetables, and cut back a bit on portion sizes overall—but they aren't big ones. And we know you're ready for change, or you wouldn't be reading this book.

The Power of Choice

Can a "self-selected" diet really control blood sugar as well as one that imposes more rigid guidelines? Researchers at Emory University in Atlanta recently put this question to the test with 648 African-Americans, whose risk of diabetes is twice that of Caucasians. One group of type 2 diabetes patients was put on an eating plan using food exchanges, while another group was given a much simpler program that emphasized making healthy choices (balanced meals, less fat) like those of the 10 Percent Plan. The result: The people in the healthy choices group improved their blood sugar just as much as those on the plan that used the food exchanges.

key principles
OF THE
plan

The 10 Percent Plan is designed to give you plenty of freedom to decide how you'll meet your weight-loss goal—but that doesn't mean the plan is totally unstructured or without guidelines. Rather, it is based on principles that make intuitive sense and are proven to help people with diabetes.

On the 10 Percent Plan, we ask you to abide by the following simple rules. Later chapters will give more details on exactly how to do it.

The good news is that you won't get a list of "thou shalt nots," because on this plan, you don't have to completely give up anything. All foods are allowed, in appropriate portion sizes. So breathe easy (in fact, it's one of the rules). These are guidelines that will inspire just about anyone to say, "Yes, I can do that."

1

eat more often

Start your day by eating breakfast, then go absolutely no more than 5 waking hours without a meal or snack.

By keeping food in your system, you avoid wild swings in blood sugar—deep valleys brought on by skipping meals or eating them late and high peaks brought on by a surge in glucose when you finally get something in your stomach. Just as important, you keep your appetite under control by not letting hunger build to the point where you're ravenous.

Eating more often means, for starters, eating breakfast every day. This not only helps keep your blood sugar levels stable, it also helps you eat fewer calories throughout the day, according to several studies. What's more, it revs up your metabolism so you burn more calories.

Research suggests that practicing this one simple habit can confer striking health benefits. For example, a report presented to the American Heart Association in 2003 found that rates of obesity and metabolic problems such as insulin resistance were 35 to 50 percent lower in people who ate breakfast.

In terms of what you eat the rest of the day, if you're planning a late lunch or dinner, you'll need to have a snack in between. That's right, on the 10 Percent Plan, we *want* you to snack. Again, the aim is to keep your blood sugar steady and never get too hungry. You'll learn how to master your meal timing in Step One of the plan.

2

RULE

eat balanced meals

Forget the question of protein versus carbohydrates. We want you to get some of both at each meal, plus at least one fruit or vegetable.

This is the best approach to controlling your blood sugar, feeling full longer, and losing weight. Sound simple? It is. Yet clinical experience suggests that if you're overweight, that's probably not the way you're eating now. In fact, your nutritional intake may be so out of balance that you may actually be deficient in certain nutrients despite the fact that you're taking in too many calories. Some nutritionists believe that the body's need for a variety of nutrients triggers your appetite in order to make sure you get them. If you simply eat more of what you always eat, your body never gets enough of what it really needs. In Step Two of the plan, we'll show you just how to make sure every meal, whether sit-down or on-the-go, contains the right balance of carbohydrates, protein, and fruits and vegetables to keep blood sugar steady and help you shed weight.

RULE 3
eat a little less of everything but vegetables

Portion control is essential to weight loss, but that doesn't mean you won't get enough to eat. On the contrary, you have permission to eat as much as you want—of vegetables.

Consider vegetables the ideal food: They're good sources of complex carbohydrates and smaller amounts of protein; they're generally low in fat and high in fiber; and they're rich in a variety of vitamins, minerals, and other nutrients. The

Secrets of Enjoyable Eating

In some quarters, the idea that you should take pleasure in food is controversial. In fact, the U.S. Dietary Guidelines changed their instruction from "enjoy a variety of foods" to "*eat* a variety of foods." But Canada's Food Guide to Healthy Eating still urges Canadians to "enjoy." Should you worry that you might *over*-enjoy? Not necessarily. Many nutrition researchers say it's better to selectively indulge your tastes for finer (read: richer) foods than to eat a bland, boring diet you'll soon tire of. Here are some ways to increase your pleasure without overindulging your appetite.

Slow the pace. The best sensual experiences are savored. By eating more slowly, you deepen your experience of flavors, better appreciate the social aspects of a meal, and give your body's appetite controls more time to signal that you're full, so you ultimately eat less.

Engage the senses. Pleasure doesn't have to mean calories. You can boost your enjoyment of a meal by appealing to senses other than taste. Examples: Buy a small bouquet of flowers or gather cuttings from your garden to brighten your table, dine by the light of a small votive candle, or play your favorite music at dinnertime.

Indulge like royalty. Choose one sinfully delicious chocolate instead of a box of fat-free cookies. The intensity and richness of the treat will make you feel satisfied, and it will actually have fewer calories than a larger portion of a "healthier" snack.

same is true of many fruits. That's why different forms of produce should fill at least half of your plate at any meal. To avoid getting too many sugars throughout the day, think of fruit primarily as a breakfast food and a dessert, but feel free to load up on vegetables anytime.

By adding more produce to your plate, you may actually eat more in terms of volume while still helping yourself lose weight. Plus, you'll leave less room for foods that constitute so much of the typical North American diet: highly processed and packaged foods, meats, sweets, starches, and fats. Are these foods forbidden? No. All foods belong in your diet, and everything is allowed. For the plan to work, though, your total intake of calories needs to decrease.

In Step Two of the plan, you'll learn how to get more vegetables on your plate. Then Step Three puts it all together with menus for breakfast, lunch, and dinner, all in the proper portion sizes.

RULE 4 trim the fat

Cut back on total fat and substitute the "right" fats for the "wrong" ones.

Fat contains more than twice the calories of carbohydrates or protein, so it's an obvious target if you're trying to lose weight. Simply by eating more vegetables, which you'll do on the 10 Percent Plan, you're likely to eat less fat. But we won't ask you to cut all the fat from your diet. In fact, studies show that eating a moderate amount of fat helps people stick to healthy diets, and some types of fat even help keep your blood sugar steady.

The key is to cut back on the "wrong" types of fat by consuming leaner meats and low-fat versions of dairy products, such as milk and cheese. That's because meat and dairy foods contain saturated fats, which contribute to insulin resistance (not to mention clogged arteries). "Good" fats, on the other hand, such as the ones in most cooking oils and in fish, actually help stabilize your blood sugar because they're digested more slowly than carbohydrates are.

In one study, women trying to cut their overall fat intake discovered that their single most effective strategy was to avoid fat as a flavoring—for example, by not slathering butter on bread or potatoes. Instead, use low-fat or fat-free versions of mayonnaise, sour cream, and salad dressing or try flavorful condiments such as pepper and chives. It's also crucial to put some of your favorite high-fat foods on a diet. In Step Four, you'll trim the fat—and calorie content—of everything from burgers to macaroni and cheese. Don't worry, though; they'll still taste great!

shake a leg

RULE 5

Start becoming more physically active by walking— just 10 minutes a day at first. Then add more time in small increments and work easy strengthening exercises into your routine.

Weight-loss experts agree that no weight-loss plan is likely to work unless it includes physical activity. In fact, many of the people in the DO IT study said that boosting their activity levels was one of the most important keys to their success. Exercise burns calories and tones the muscles. It also boosts your muscle cells' insulin sensitivity, making your body more efficient at using glucose and thereby lowering your blood sugar. What's more, people who exercise have better luck keeping weight off in the long term than people who simply watch what they eat. And exercise feels good! In Step Five, you'll get your body in motion with simple activities such as walking, stretching, and gentle strength training.

learn to relax

RULE 6

Stress does more than wrinkle your brow—it raises your blood sugar as well. We want you to attack the problem with simple, soothing relaxation strategies and mood-calming mental techniques.

When you're feeling stressed, your body releases hormones that rev it up and prepare it to fight or flee. The same hormones also raise blood sugar. Recent groundbreaking research shows that you can significantly lower your blood sugar by getting stress under control. In fact, stress-reduction techniques can work almost as well as some diabetes medications. In Step Six, we'll help you manage stress, anxiety, and hostility by meditating, breathing, relaxing your muscles, practicing mental imagery exercises, and more. We'll also show how to keep your emotions from making you overeat as well as how to improve your mood—and your blood sugar—by getting better sleep.

7 RULE track your progress

It doesn't make sense to follow the plan and not check to see if it's working. Monitoring your progress won't take the weight off directly, but it will provide encouragement when you see positive results and let you know that something's not working if you don't.

It's also important to record your efforts to exercise more and eat better. Studies show that people who write down what they eat are more likely to consume fewer calories. And we have a strong feeling that people who track their exercise efforts are more likely to stick to a get-moving plan (like the one in this book).

Starting on page 208, you'll find logs to help you keep track of your weight, your blood sugar, your exercise, and your diet. (You'll read more about tracking your weight and your food intake in "Before You Begin" on page 28.)

How often you need to test your blood sugar depends on several factors. You should work out a testing schedule with your doctor. As a general guideline, though, if you don't take medication or insulin and your blood sugar tends to stay in a relatively stable range between 5 and 7 mmol/L, you may be able to test just a few times per week. But count on testing at least three times a week at the start of the program, preferably in the morning before you've had anything to eat. Your doctor may also want you to test again before dinner for an idea of how your blood sugar changes during the day. If your blood sugar swings higher into the abnormal range, follow your doctor's advice for testing more often. If you're on insulin, medication, or both, you may need to test three or four times a day, typically before meals and perhaps at bedtime.

before you begin

You're probably eager to start the 10 Percent Plan right away. That's terrific, because if you have a positive attitude, you're halfway there. Before you officially dive in, though, take a few minutes to make sure you're really ready to go.

Here you'll take stock of your current health, determine your weight-loss goal, and analyze your current diet to reveal your biggest pitfalls and discover your biggest opportunities for improvement.

You'll also find out how to go about following the 10 Percent Plan. The answer: By making small changes over time. It's the most effective way to lose weight—and lower your blood sugar—safely and permanently. You can't overhaul your lifestyle overnight, and you shouldn't expect to. Remember, the 10 Percent Plan is an approach you'll follow for the rest of your life.

Take Stock of Your Health

The 10 Percent Plan is for anyone who has type 2 diabetes or is at risk for it, but of course, everyone is unique. Your weight-loss target in terms of the number of kilograms (or pounds) you want to lose will be different from the next person's. Likewise, factors such as whether you're on oral medication or insulin and how long you've had diabetes will influence your goals. One person may have the goal of getting off medication, another may hope to avoid starting medication, and a third may have to stay on medication but want to lower the dose. Finally, some people may have health issues that require caution when it comes to certain types of exercise.

Before you start Step One of the 10 Percent Plan, take a few minutes to define your weight-loss goals and make sure you have all the information you need about your blood sugar levels as well as your ability to exercise safely.

Do You Have Diabetes?

Many Canadians have diabetes but don't know they have it. Not sure if you're among them? Symptoms such as extreme thirst, frequent urination, and unexplained weight loss are blatant warnings. Even if you don't have diabetes, you may be at risk for developing it if you:

- Are overweight
- Are age 65 or older or are younger than 65 and don't exercise regularly
- Ever gave birth to a baby weighing more than 4 kg (9 lb)
- Have a sibling or parent with diabetes

Go online to download the questionnaire "Are You at Risk?" on the Canadian Diabetes Association website at www.diabetes.ca.

FIND YOUR 10 PERCENT TARGET

First, figure out what you weigh now. (That's simple enough.) Next, calculate your 10 percent goal by multiplying your current weight by 0.10; that will tell you how much weight you'll aim to lose. (For example, if you weigh 100 kg [220 lb], you'd multiply 100 by 0.10 to get 10 kg [220 x 0.10 = 22 lb].) Finally, subtract this number from your current weight to find your target weight. Plan to get there gradually, your time frame is six months. In most cases, that amounts to losing about 0.5 kg (1 lb) per week—a very doable goal.

Why not aim higher (or should we say lower)? Studies find that people who are trying to lose weight often have unrealistic expectations that are self-defeating because they lead to disappointment. By sticking to a 10 percent weight-loss goal, you'll have a better chance of succeeding. And it's no small success: Doctors know that the first 5 to 10 percent of body weight lost has proportionately the biggest effect on blood pressure, cholesterol, and glucose levels.

See "What's Your Goal?" for a sample of weight-loss goals in the 10 Percent Plan, computed for different starting weights.

KNOW YOUR BLOOD SUGAR LEVELS

Before you start the 10 Percent Plan, schedule a visit with your doctor. When you see him, make sure you get a fasting plasma glucose test to establish your current baseline blood sugar levels. Many people on the 10 Percent Plan can expect a drop of about 25 percent in fasting blood glucose. Depending on where your blood sugar levels are now, that could be enough to get you off medication or even bring your blood sugar back into the normal range.

In addition to the fasting plasma glucose test, there's another you should have: a hemoglobin A1C test, which indicates what your average blood sugar levels have been over the course of the past two to three months. If you're not already taking this test every three to six months, you should be. Assuming you've had an A1C test within the past three months, and nothing about your blood sugar levels or treatment has changed, use that reading as your baseline for the 10 Percent Plan. After you start the plan, figure on taking another test in about three months to see if your levels have changed.

what's your goal?

IF YOU WEIGH KG/LB*	YOUR 10% TARGET WEIGHT IS KG/LB*	FOR A LOSS OF KG/LB*
70/150	63/135	7/15
75/160	67.5/144	7.5/16
80/170	72/153	8/17
85/180	76.5/162	8.5/18
90/190	81/171	9/19
95/200	85.5/180	9.5/20
100/210	90/189	10/21
105/220	94.5/198	10.5/22
110/230	99/207	11/23
115/240	103.5/216	11.5/24
120/250	108/225	12/25
125/260	112.5/234	12.5/26
130/270	117/243	13/27
135/280	121.5/252	13.5/28
140/290	126/261	14/29
145/300	130.5/270	14.5/30

* Not intended as equivalents.

While you're on the plan, it's important to keep close tabs on your blood sugar levels by using a home glucose monitor, not only to see how well the plan is working but also to help prevent a potential side effect of success: hypoglycemia. When you start to lose weight and exercise more, your blood sugar levels will probably drop—after all, that's the point of the plan! But you don't want them to drop dangerously low, especially between meals or after exercise. That's why you need to stay in close communication with your doctor, so he can lower your dose of medication or insulin when it's appropriate.

ASK ABOUT EXERCISE

While you're at the doctor's office, discuss your exercise plans. Tell your doctor you'll be walking more in the near future, as well as doing some gentle stretches and strengthening exercises, and ask whether anything about your current health is cause for concern. For example, if you show signs of poor blood flow or nerve damage (neuropathy), you'll want to pay special attention to your feet, since these problems can make you oblivious to injuries that can quickly become serious. Does that mean you should avoid walking? Not necessarily, but you may need to take precautions, such as buying a better pair of shoes or using moisturizing cream to keep the skin on your feet from cracking.

People with diabetes also need to be aware of their increased risk for heart problems. Again, light activity such as walking is unlikely to cause any trouble and is actually an excellent way to protect your heart—but if moderate activity causes shortness of breath or chest pain, for example, your doctor may want to follow your progress more closely. He may even ask you to take an exercise stress test before you start exercising if you have diabetes and meet any of the following criteria.

- You're over age 35
- You're over age 25 and have had type 2 diabetes for more than 10 years

Engineering Expectations

Setting your sights on a 10 percent loss has an advantage over most other weight-loss plans—even those with more aggressive goals. In fact, weight loss is one area in which ambition can work against you. The fact is that many people have unrealistic expectations that can easily lead to disappointment. In one study, researchers asked 60 obese women to define their goal weight and four others: their "dream" weight, "happy" weight, "acceptable" weight, and "disappointed" weight. In the course of a 48-week weight-loss treatment, the women lost an average of 16 kg (35 lb) and reported a variety of physical and psychological benefits. Yet almost half had not reached their "disappointed" weight, and only 9 percent had reached their "happy" weight.

Satisfaction requires a match between what you expect and what you get. A realistic short-term goal is losing 0.5 kg (1 lb) a week. If you succeed in losing that amount, congratulate yourself—then keep going!

- You have any other risk factor for heart disease, such as high blood pressure or a poor cholesterol profile
- You've already been diagnosed or show signs of poor blood flow in your limbs, such as pain in your calves or buttocks
- You've already been diagnosed or show signs of nerve damage, such as tingling or numbness

Analyze Your Current Diet

"Dear Diary: Today I had one sausage biscuit and a 340-ml (12-oz) cup of coffee for breakfast." All right, these aren't exactly secrets that sizzle off the page—unless the sizzle is the sound of your hidden yen for greasy meat. But a food diary *can* make interesting reading (for you, anyway) because it can be so revealing.

Don't take our word for it: Keep one yourself. It's the only way to get an accurate picture of your real eating habits—and that's important to do before you start trying to change them.

Most people think they have a pretty good idea of what they eat. When it comes to meal memory and snack recall, though, we're all too prone to senior moments. As an experiment, see if you can you remember everything you ate in the evening a week ago yesterday. "Well," you tell yourself, "it was a night like any other." You got home, made dinner, and relaxed with a magazine. But rewind to making dinner. What if your meal preparations began with opening a bag of chips? What if you constantly nibbled on the dinner ingredients as you put them together? What if you ate leftovers from the pan to keep from washing storage containers? Just one week of food diary entries would reveal whether you often eat "extra" food while preparing meals and uncover hidden calories that you eat more out of habit than hunger.

The better you understand the way you're really eating right now, the better you'll be able to identify your biggest downfalls—and your biggest opportunities for improvement. If you see in hard numbers how many calories you blow on potato chips every day, for instance, it's an inspiration to switch to fruit, yogurt, or pretzels instead. If gobbling leftovers during meal clean-up is your Achilles' heel, see it as a great excuse to recruit your kids for the chore.

Weight loss is all about choices like these that we make every day, and the choices you *can* make become clearer in light of the choices you *do* make.

WHAT TO RECORD

First, make seven photocopies of the food log on page 210, then use them to keep track of everything you eat for seven days. (That way, you'll be sure to include both weekdays and weekends, when eating habits are often quite different.) You can either carry the form with you wherever you go or use a small notepad to record what you eat when you're not at home, then transfer the information to the form later.

Sample Daily Food Diary

TIME	WHAT I ATE	PORTION	NOTES	CALORIES
7 a.m.	Coffee with 2 sugars	1 cup	Wake up! Didn't sleep enough	35
7:30 a.m.	Cornflakes w/	2 cups	The usual	200
	2% milk	1 cup		120
	Orange juice	1 cup		110
8:30 a.m.	Éclair	1	Jim brought a box of	280
			goodies to office	
	Coffee with 2 sugars	1 cup	At desk	35
10 a.m.	Coffee with 2 sugars	1 cup	Meeting	35
	Chocolate donut	1	Remaining goodies from box	235
			brought to meeting	
1 p.m.	Ham and cheese	1	Lunch	360
	sandwich on roll w/			
	lettuce and 2 slices tomato			
	Single-serving chips	28 g (1 oz)		160
	Diet cola	340 ml (12 oz)		0
3:15 p.m.	Candy bar	56 g (2 oz)	Hit the vending machine	270
7:30 p.m.	Frozen pizza	3 slices	Too tired and late to make	570
			a real meal	
	Beer	340 ml (12 oz)		150
7:45 p.m.	Pizza	1 slice	Last piece not worth wrapping	190
10 p.m.	Apple pie w/	1 slice	Bedtime snack	395
	vanilla ice cream	1 cup		265
	TOTAL CALORIES			3,410

Don't worry whether your eating fits into a particular meal; just make a note of what you actually put in your mouth—and that means *every* item. Did you grab a handful of breakfast cereal on your way out the door? Write it down. Did you take a chocolate from the box when your coworker passed it around? Did you nibble while preparing dinner? Record every morsel. Include beverages and add-ons such as salad dressing, salsa, gravy, and butter.

A quick but important aside: Your goal during this for-the-record week is to eat normally. Don't eat as if you're starting a diet or trying to "be good," although it may be tempting to make your habits look better than they really are. When you record what you eat, also record:

- The time. This will shed light on patterns in your meals and nibbling.
- Estimated portions. See "A Visual Guide to Portion Sizes" on page 85 for help.
- Notes about circumstances, such as "popcorn at the movies" or "coffee with a neighbor," or how you were feeling, such as "angry because I got into an argument with my spouse."

Sample Food Diary: A Quick Critique

In the sample food diary on page 33, take a look at that calorie count—it's about double what it should be if you want to lose weight. So what went wrong? Not everything: Lunch, for example, is a good, low-calorie choice, as is the diet soft drink. But most of this person's meals and snacks could use a makeover. The problem areas:

- There are few vegetables and whole grains: Aside from lettuce and tomato in the sandwich, this person's choices are almost entirely processed foods with lots of fat, refined carbohydrates, or both. Whole wheat bread would have been an improvement over the roll.
- Each packet of sugar in the coffee adds 16 calories, a total of 96 for the day. Switching to artificial sweetener would save more than 35,000 calories a year.
- This person tends to eat whatever is available—whether it's doughnuts, pizza, or a candy bar. More mindful choices could cut calories significantly.
- Eating a single-serving bag of chips is a good strategy, but choosing a lower-fat snack would cut calories.
- Pizza is okay now and then, but this person should have stopped at two pieces and could have gotten some vegetables by adding them on top.
- 10 P.M. is late to be putting away more food—especially foods that are high in both calories and fat.

Observations like these can show your relationship with food and reveal why you eat as well as what and when.

At the end of each day, sit down and figure out how many calories each item provided. How? Packaged foods have calorie counts on their nutrition labels. Just be sure to check how many servings the package contains (what looks like a single serving might in fact be two) and estimate how much of it you ate. For fresh foods, you'll need a calorie counter. These books are available at bookstores or the library, or you can log on to an online calorie counter from organizations such as the Calorie Control Council (www.caloriecontrol.org). Once you've figured out the calories for each item, calculate your daily total.

If this process seems overly tedious, don't worry too much about it: You'll find that writing down what and when you eat is valuable even without the calorie counts. At this point, though, the more information you have, the better.

REVIEWING YOUR FOOD DIARY

At the end of the week, put on your detective's hat and look over your diary for "clues" to your eating habits. Just through the act of writing everything down, you've probably already come to some surprising conclusions. To learn more, follow your answers down each of the columns and see if you can detect patterns. Chances are, your eating isn't willy-nilly, even if it feels that way sometimes. Consider the following:

TIME. Do you tend to eat late at night or go a long time without eating? (Remember, on the 10 Percent Plan, we want you to eat breakfast within 2 hours of getting up and never go more than 5 hours without a meal or small snack. You'll read more about timing in Step One.) Do you eat the majority of your food in the second half of the day? Does the time of day dictate the food you eat—for example, junk in the late afternoon because that's all you can get from the vending machine?

FOODS. We often eat without really thinking. You may be convinced that you eat a lot of fresh vegetables and only occasional sweets, but your record may show otherwise. Notice what categories most of your foods fall into. Do you eat a lot of processed foods (think foods that come in a box), snack foods, fried foods, or takeout? Do you favor carbohydrates (breads, pasta, rice, and cereal) or protein (meat, poultry, cheese, and soy), or do you get some of each at every meal? Are vegetables anywhere to be seen in your food diary? Keep this information in mind. It will come in handy when you read about the Plate Approach in Step Two.

ESTIMATED PORTION. How much pasta or cereal do you eat at one sitting? Do you tend to go overboard only on certain foods (your favorite chicken and biscuits dish, for example)? Do you always finish an item once you've started eating? You may never have thought much about portion sizes before you started your food diary, and perhaps you're eating more than you realized. The key to success depends on eating appropriate portions. On the 10 Percent Plan, you'll be much more deliberate about how large your servings are. You'll read more about portion sizes—and discover a week's worth of properly portioned meals—in Step Three.

NOTES. What's going on—and how do you feel—when you reach for food, especially outside of mealtimes? Are you with friends? Watching TV? Stressed out? Bored? In many cases, circumstances have more to do with what, when, and how much we eat than whether or not we're hungry. As you go forward, keep tabs on what situations make you eat more or eat badly.

CALORIES. Take a look at your daily calorie counts. What food makes the biggest dent in your daily tally? Calories can be sneaky because a food's volume has little to do with how many calories it contains. Who would guess that a handful of mixed nuts has the same number of calories as a 3.6-kg (8-lb) watermelon? If you haven't filled in the calorie counts on your chart, think about doing it now—and look for calorie bombs that you can defuse. You may be surprised by how little it takes to shave substantial calories from the choices you typically make. Let's say fried chicken is one of your favorite dishes. Just by switching from a fried chicken thigh (240 calories) to a roasted skinless chicken breast (140 calories), you'll save 100 calories. On the 10 Percent Plan, you'll learn many ways to trim your total calorie intake, sometimes by preparing a food differently and sometimes by eating a little less of it.

We won't ask you to hit a particular calorie goal on the plan, but if you want to know how your current calorie intake compares with recommended targets for weight loss, women who are trying to lose weight are typically advised to get around 1,400 calories a day, and men are advised to get 1,600 to 1,800.

quiz
Dissecting Your Food Diary

Check your food diary to help you answer the following questions. For each, circle the number to the left of the answer that best reflects your choices.

1. I eat breakfast:
1 Hardly ever
2 Off and on
3 Every day

2. Between meals, I:
1 Don't eat anything at all
2 Always have at least one large snack
3 Have a light snack if I feel hungry

3. I eat the most:
1 At dinner and throughout the evening
2 At lunch and throughout the afternoon
3 In the morning and at lunch

4. At lunch and dinner, I:
1 Rarely eat vegetables with my meal
2 Sometimes have a vegetable
3 Almost always have at least one vegetable or a salad

5. I eat fruit:
1 Seldom
2 A few times a week
3 One to three times a day

6. When I eat a carbohydrate food, it tends to be:
1 French fries or sugared cereals
2 White bread, pasta, white rice, or mashed potatoes
3 Whole grain breads and cereals or starchy beans, such as navy or kidney beans

7. Most of the foods I eat tend to be:
1 Fast food or takeout (Chinese, pizza)
2 Processed foods (packaged foods, frozen dinners)
3 Fresh (fruit, vegetables, meals cooked at home using fresh ingredients)

8. My biggest sources of calories are:
1 Sweets or snack foods
2 Meat and potatoes
3 Vegetables, fruits, and whole grains

9. When I drink beverages, I prefer:
1 Regular soda
2 Fruit juice
3 Diet soda or water

10. I eat sweets such as cookies, cakes, and candy:
1 More than once a day
2 About once a day
3 Less than once a day

11. The meats I eat the most tend to be:
1 Hot dogs, sausage, ribs, chicken wings, bacon, or salami
2 Chicken or turkey legs, ground chuck, T-bone steak, or chuck roast
3 Ground sirloin, beef or pork tenderloin, skinless chicken or turkey breast, lean ham, or fresh fish

12. My meals consist of the same foods:
1 Four or more times a week
2 Three times a week
3 One or two times a week or less

Tally your score, then turn the page.

quiz
What Your Score Means

27 to 36: Your eating habits are already pretty good. So why are you overweight? Chances are, your portion sizes are too big (see Step Three) or you aren't getting enough exercise (see Step Five).

18 to 26: You're off to a good start, but your eating habits could use some improvement. What changes should you make? Look back at your answers. Did you circle any 1s? Check out the comments on those questions below to see how the 10 Percent Plan will help you.

12 to 17: You tend to make poor food choices, but that means you have the most to gain from even small improvements. Review your answers: Did you answer any with 3s or 2s? These are successes: Give yourself credit, and make more 3s and 2s your goal.

The logic behind the questions:

1. Research shows that people who eat breakfast have better luck losing weight—and the right breakfast will help keep your blood sugar steady for hours.

2. Going without food for more than 5 hours makes you ravenous and leads to overeating. You'll learn that it's okay to snack between meals if you keep portions small.

3. Eating a big dinner and noshing into the night piles on calories when your metabolism is slowest. Getting most of your calories early in the day is smarter.

4. Vegetables are going to fill the biggest part of your plate in the 10 Percent Plan because they're powerfully nutritious and filling without adding many calories.

5. Fruits provide lots of nutrients and fiber, so it's good to eat some daily. Because fruits have more calories and sugar than vegetables, you should have no more than four servings a day.

6. Carbohydrates aren't necessarily bad for people with diabetes, but some carbohydrates are better than others. Whole grains and beans help steady your blood sugar, while refined carbs (think white bread and white pasta) and sugar make it swing.

7. Fresh foods tend to have more nutrients and far less fat, calories, and sodium than processed foods or fast food.

8. Knowing where you take your biggest calorie hits is your first step toward cutting back on foods that add weight.

9. Beverages—even fruit juice—can be a surprisingly significant source of empty calories. Switching to diet drinks or water can make a big difference to your waistline.

10. Sweets are okay, in moderation. We'll help you switch to lower-sugar sweets and healthier treats and snacks.

11. Some meats are very high in fat. Choosing leaner cuts saves you calories and cuts back on saturated fat, the kind that decreases insulin sensitivity.

12. Variety is the spice of life. If you eat the same things over and over again, you'd better make sure they're good for you. It's better to vary your meals as much as possible.

Following the 10 Percent Plan

By now, you probably have a pretty good idea of what to expect on the 10 Percent Plan. Maybe you're asking yourself, "When do I start?" and "When do the payoffs begin?" The answer to both questions? Today.

On the 10 Percent Plan, each day should be a small victory—and each small victory should bolster your efforts to win another. Soon—how soon depends on you—those little triumphs will start showing up on the scale and in your blood sugar readings.

There's no set timetable on the 10 Percent Plan and no pressure to drop huge amounts of weight at once. In fact, we don't want you to rush into big changes right out of the starting gate. Instead, the idea is to make slow and steady progress at a pace that seems right for you.

Start by making one change—such as eating whole grain cereal for breakfast or having more vegetables at dinner—and try to stick with that new habit for a few days, a week, or even two weeks before you try to make another change. Each planned improvement in your eating or exercise habits should make you think, "That's no big deal." Can you eat a mini-bagel instead of a full-size one? (No problem.) Can you take a 10-minute stroll most days? (Don't see why not.) Can you throw a cup of frozen mixed vegetables into your soup? (You call this a diet?) Changes like these can—and should—seem almost trivial. As you keep piling them on, though, they add up to differences that *are* a big deal.

This is a radically different approach from weight-loss plans that make you change your eating habits overnight. We don't need to cite studies (although there are plenty out there) to show what you probably know from your own experience: Dramatic diets can produce dramatic results, but they feel too much like work. The next thing you know, you're tired of them and go back to your old ways—and those dramatic results evaporate.

The 10 Percent Plan, on the other hand, provides a solution for life. It starts with what you eat now and how much you currently exercise, then makes small tweaks here and there—and keeps making them—until you've lost weight and lowered your blood sugar. How could one change make you lose weight? The answer is, it won't—by itself. But that one change (eating strawberries with fat-free whipped topping instead of ice cream, for example) will *start* to make you lose weight. With each passing day, you'll feel more successful, motivated, and able to compound your efforts with more changes. It's like the proverbial bank account that starts with just $1 and doubles every day: In 21 days, that dollar makes you a millionaire.

What happens after you've lost 10 percent of your body weight? Nothing changes. You keep on doing exactly what you've been doing. If you want to lose more weight, you can look for more small victories to win based on the principles of the 10 Percent Plan.

We've organized the plan into steps, but there's no real need to follow them in order. If you're willing to start walking tomorrow, feel free to skip ahead to Step Five. If stress-related eating is a major problem for you, you may want to start with Step Six. Even if you start at the beginning with Step One, you'll find "Fast Track" tips (like the ones on the opposite page) to give you a jump-start on the steps to come.

TRACKING YOUR WEIGHT

While you're on the 10 Percent Plan, you'll want to weigh yourself consistently and accurately. Hint: That doesn't mean stepping on the scale four times a day. The best approach is as follows.

- Weigh yourself in the morning. Your baseline weight is most accurately determined first thing in the morning, after you've used the toilet but before you've eaten or dressed.

- No matter how anxious you are to see progress, don't weigh yourself more than once a day. Weight can fluctuate by as much as 2.3 kg (5 lb) during the course of a day. Using that morning reading alone guards against the potential frustration of getting a later reading that seems to make your progress evaporate.

- Expect progress to vary. Clinical experience with thousands of people, including those in the DO IT study, suggests that after four to five weeks of steady losses, your weight might rise slightly. After that, the pattern will probably be one of losses followed by smaller upward blips. Don't be discouraged by these periodic gains as your metabolism

The Fast Track

On the 10 Percent Plan, you'll eat a little less, never let yourself get too hungry, and sneak more physical activity into your day. To see how easy it can be, do these four things today.

Eat a High-Fiber Breakfast

Breakfast is a critical element of the plan because research suggests that people who start the day with a well-balanced meal do better at controlling blood sugar and losing weight. The best breakfasts contain significant amounts of fiber, which slows digestion, helps you feel full on fewer calories, and slows the rise of blood sugar after a meal. Try one of these.

- 1 cup oatmeal; ¼ cup craisins or ½ cup sliced strawberries; ½ cup fat-free milk (6 g fiber, 325 calories)

- 1 cup sugar-free, fat-free yogurt topped with 1 tablespoon high-fiber bran cereal; ½ cup fresh berries, melon, or mixed fruit (7 g fiber, 230 calories)

- 2 slices whole wheat toast topped with 2 tablespoons chunky peanut butter; 1 medium banana (10 g fiber, 465 calories)

Take a 5-Minute Walk

You don't have to set aside an hour for a workout in order to start becoming more active. All it takes is a commitment of 5 minutes—long enough for a quick walk. Small jaunts easily work into the business of daily life and require so little time, they're hardly worth calling a commitment. Nevertheless, the mere act of putting one foot in front of the other gets you in the habit of moving. You could, for example:

- Walk a child to the bus stop.

- Enter a mall through the doors farthest from your destination.

- Go to the corner mailbox rather than putting the letter in your own box.

Check the TV Schedule

The average Canadian watches almost 4 hours of TV a day. Chances are, you stare at the glare because the TV just happens to be on. Today, check the schedule and decide ahead of time what you want to see, then watch only that. This should free substantial chunks of time that you can use for more active pursuits. The link between TV viewing and weight is striking: A recent study from Australia found that people who watched TV for 2½ to 4 hours a day were 183 percent more likely to be overweight than people who watched for less than an hour.

Pick One Food and Eat a Little Less of It

For weight loss, what you eat may matter less than how much of it you eat. With the 10 Percent Plan, you'll work on eating fewer calories than you do now. Sometimes you'll be able to do this by making substitutions, but some foods just can't be replaced. Instead of giving them up, eat less of them. If you love bacon, eat two strips instead of three. If you enjoy a milkshake with lunch, request an extra glass and share.

adjusts—they're normal. Keep your eyes on the big picture: If the overall weight trend is down, you're succeeding.

It's also important to keep in mind that if you've started exercising more (as you will when you get to Step Five), you may be adding muscle, which weighs more than fat. Thus, while your clothes may begin to fit better and your pants button more easily, you may not notice much weight loss right away. Be patient; the muscle tissue you're adding will speed your metabolism and ultimately help you lose more weight.

ADJUSTING YOUR MEDICATION

If you're currently on medication to bring your blood sugar down, you'll probably be able to adjust your dose once you start losing weight. Of course, you'll need to make that decision in consultation with your doctor. As you proceed with the plan, monitor your blood sugar regularly and keep your doctor abreast of any changes. (If you don't already have a blood sugar log, use the one on page 213.)

Are You Ready?

Trying to lose weight now probably means that you've tried it before. Studies find that the attitudes and psychological baggage you carry from previous attempts can affect how well you do today—but only if you let them. Do you have the right attitudes to succeed? Look at the following checklist and mark all the statements you agree with.

❑ The best way to lose weight is slowly and gradually, not all at once.

❑ Achieving a weight loss of 10 percent is a major accomplishment that will have a significant impact on my health.

❑ I'm willing to make small adjustments in my dietary habits as long as I can eat foods I like.

❑ I'm certain there are ways I can work more physical activity into my life without too much trouble.

❑ Two steps forward and one step back is still progress.

❑ I don't want to be on a diet—I want to permanently change the way I eat.

❑ Diets haven't worked for me, but it's still possible for me to lose weight.

The more checkmarks you placed next to these statements, the more certain you can be that you have the right spirit to make this plan work for you. The next question is when to start—but that implies that you need to wait for some magic moment, like the sound of a starter's pistol or the word "Go!" for permission to cross the line. Don't wait! You can begin making small changes *right now*.

Beyond saving money and sparing you potential side effects, cutting back on medication may actually help you lose weight. The reason: Losing weight and getting more exercise will cause your blood sugar to drop. If you don't lower your dose of medication, your glucose levels may drop so low that you'll be tempted to overeat.

How you adjust your medication will depend on how much your blood sugar levels vary, your history of hypoglycemia, which medications you take and at what doses, and how much you're exercising. As a rule, moderate exercise isn't likely to cause blood sugar to crash, but it's not uncommon for exercisers at the start of a program to feel "shaky" or "weird" after a bout of activity. These effects can easily be overcome by eating a small amount of a sugary food, such as four Lifesaver candies; drinking a half-cup of a regular soft drink; or popping a glucose tab specially made for this purpose. But there's a natural tendency to take this "permission" to eat a little too far—often by having, say, a whole piece of pie or an entire meal—and that won't do your weight-loss efforts any good.

CONTINUING YOUR FOOD DIARY

We're not going to insist that you keep a food diary indefinitely, but if you're serious about succeeding, it's something you should consider. Studies have shown that people who continually keep tabs on their eating habits—in writing—are more likely to eat fewer calories and lose weight than those who don't. And in cases where both record keepers and non-record keepers drop pounds, the note takers lose more.

"Even when traveling, I'd carry a piece of paper in my jacket pocket to write on," says Vince Petroy, who lowered his blood sugar to normal from the high teens during the DO IT study. "I'd jot down what I ate and fill in the log later in my hotel room. It wasn't a big production. In fact, it was a good conversation piece."

If you hate the idea of keeping a food log, and it becomes a roadblock to staying on the plan, it's better to ditch the diary, but even writing down what you eat 50 to 75 percent of the time has been shown to make a measurable difference in weight loss.

tion

(so•lu•tion) *noun*

1. A homogeneous mixture of
two or more substances.

2. A set of values that satisfies
an equation.

3. The answer to a problem.
The 10 Percent Plan is your
solution to high blood sugar.

PART TWO

The 10 Percent Plan

STEP 1
master your timing

It's true in love, war, business, comedy—and weight loss: Timing is everything. Just by watching when you eat, you can go a long way toward stabilizing your blood sugar as well as preventing your body from storing food as fat.

The beauty of the 10 Percent Plan is that we want you to eat more often, not less.

Contrary to what you might think, it's the best way to lose weight, and it helps keep glucose swings in check. So bring on breakfast! Bring on the snacks!

When you have diabetes, eating is a little like riding a roller coaster. Meals spaced far apart are the scariest coasters, with steep climbs followed by huge drops. By eating more often, you put the "bumps" closer together, so the peaks are lower and the dips are shallower—closer to what people with normal blood sugar experience. It's an easy way to feel better, weigh less, and take charge of your diabetes.

Most diet plans focus on *what* you eat. With the 10 Percent Plan, we want you to think first about *when* you eat. You may not think of timing as a critical part of a successful weight-loss effort—and that's exactly why it's often overlooked. The truth is that poor timing of meals is one of the biggest trouble spots for overweight people with diabetes, but it's actually good news because it's such an easy problem to correct.

What's the issue with timing? Consider the typical approach to slimming down. If you want to eat fewer calories, the reasoning goes, you should eat less often. Fewer meals means less food—right? Wrong. Skipping meals or going long periods without eating backfires in the long run. That's been proven in studies and large surveys, and you may even have discovered it firsthand. Sure, eating less often means that you temporarily avoid calories you would otherwise have eaten—but those calories tend to show up with a vengeance when you become so hungry you eat everything in sight. In addition, and just as important for people with diabetes, missing meals makes your blood sugar levels fluctuate more erratically. That's why two core rules of this plan are:

- Eat within 2 hours of getting up each morning.
- Go absolutely no more than 5 hours without eating a meal or light snack.

If you're a person who zips out the door without food in the morning or lets yourself go so long without eating that your stomach whines and growls for food, you need to pay particular attention to this advice.

Help!

My blood sugar is sky-high in the morning. Shouldn't I skip breakfast to bring it down?

No. It's true that for some people with diabetes, blood sugar tends to be high in the morning. That's because as dawn approaches, your body starts releasing energizing hormones to rev you up for the day. These antagonize the action of insulin and stimulate the liver to produce more glucose, even if the glucose level in the blood is already abnormally high. Will eating make it rise even higher? Probably, but because breakfast is so important for weight loss and proper nutrition, you need to make eating a priority and find other ways to deal with the "dawn phenomenon."

Start checking your blood sugar at 7 A.M. If it's often above 11, try controlling the morning spikes by taking action the night before. For instance, you could eat less in the evening or try exercising before you go to bed, which siphons glucose from the blood into the muscles for hours afterward. If you're taking insulin, you may also need your doctor to adjust the timing or amount of your last dose of the day. Or you may need a morning dose of medication (taken with food) to keep blood sugar under control until proper eating, exercise, and stress management get you on a more even keel.

Treat Yourself to Breakfast

Begin with the first rule: Eat within 2 hours of getting up. Actually, the 2-hour mark is pushing it—that's the absolute maximum time you should wait before eating. It's better to consider eating within the first hour to be your real goal, with an extra hour of leeway if your morning gets out of control.

Research at Harvard University has linked eating breakfast with lower rates of both obesity and insulin resistance. And in a survey of successful dieters conducted by the U.S. National Weight Control Registry, an impressive 78 percent say they eat breakfast every day, while only a minuscule 4 percent say they never do.

Starting your day with a bite to eat is a good idea even if you don't have diabetes or need to lose weight. The most obvious reason is that your body needs fuel after going many hours without nourishment, and eating breakfast tops off your tank so you feel more energetic and alert. But that's not all. Getting breakfast into your system kicks your calorie-burning furnace into gear and keeps it burning hot throughout the morning. Otherwise, it will stay on "low" because your body turns it down while you sleep to conserve energy. Eating breakfast gives your body permission to turn up the thermostat so you burn the calories from your morning meal (assuming the portions are reasonable; more on that in Step Three), and the coals stay hot so you're more likely to burn stored fat.

Eating a healthy breakfast—especially one that contains whole grains, such as wheat or bran cereal—also seems to make it easier to choose healthier foods all day long. Studies confirm that breakfast eaters are better able to resist fatty and high-calorie foods. Need more inspiration? Consider this: In a study from Vanderbilt University in Nashville, overweight women

Shake Breakfast Up

Although not officially part of the 10 Percent Plan, commercially produced meal-in-a-can products have helped many people with diabetes get over the hurdle of making breakfast a habit. The advantage: They're fast, convenient, and formulated to provide balanced nutrition. Slim-Fast and Ensure shakes are two options, but a better bet may be Glucerna nutritional drinks and bars. They are specially made for people with diabetes and contain a blend of slowly digested carbohydrates, dietary fiber, and fructose, the simple carb that makes fruit sweet. They don't cause blood sugar to rise as fast or as high as other products.

One 250-ml can of a Glucerna nutritional drink weighs in at only 230 calories—small by breakfast standards—and flavors include vanilla, chocolate, and strawberry. Or if you prefer something solid in your stomach, try a 41-g, 150-calorie meal replacement bar. You'll find Glucerna products at your local drugstore.

An Eggs-treme Speed Breakfast

Got a minute? That's about all you need to cook up a hot egg sandwich that you can carry out the door with you. Here's how.

- Crack an egg into a saucer, break the yolk, and whisk it with a fork.
- Microwave the egg on high for 30 seconds, take it out and whisk again to keep the edges from overcooking, then nuke it for another 30 seconds.
- Serve your perfectly formed egg on toast. Note: You'll want to pop the bread into the toaster before starting the egg—so they're ready at the same time.

who usually skipped breakfast started eating it every morning, and after three months, they had lost an average of 1.8 kg (4 lb) more than women in a group that didn't eat breakfast.

BREAKING IN A BREAKFAST ROUTINE

If you're not used to eating in the morning, relax: Breakfast is easier to prepare than any other meal. There's no need to dig out the mixing bowl, griddle, and skillet for pancakes, waffles, or bacon. (Those aren't ideal breakfast foods anyway—although you can have them if they're prepared and portioned to keep calories low.) In fact, the simpler you keep breakfast, the more likely you'll be to eat the best kinds of foods, such as raw fruit and whole grain cereals. How do you start?

PUT EATING FIRST. Try to have breakfast shortly after getting out of bed. That way, you'll eat before you remember that you have to take out the trash, walk the dog, pay bills, or do any other distracting tasks that can gobble up your time.

CARVE OUT MOMENTS TO MUNCH. You may be rushing out the door without grabbing a bite more out of a frantic need to beat the clock than from a misguided desire to avoid calories. The best bet for making sure you have time to eat? Set your alarm 15 minutes earlier, then be sure to go to bed at least 15 minutes earlier at night. The last thing you want to do when you have diabetes is shortchange yourself on sleep (more on that in Step Six). If possible, try to get up before the rest of the family: It's easier to make sure you feed yourself when you don't have to deal with kids who drag their feet, live-in parents who need care, spouses, or others who may demand your time and attention.

PACK IT IN. If you find it's impossible to work in a sit-down breakfast before you barrel out the door, don't sweat it. There are plenty of foods that are perfect for stuffing in a bag or briefcase. (See "Grab-and-Go Menu.")

REDEFINE BREAKFAST. Some people with diabetes say they just don't like breakfast. In many cases, what they really mean is that they don't like traditional breakfast foods—but who says breakfast has to be eggs, toast, or cereal? As long as your body gets a mix of protein and carbohydrate, it doesn't matter what you eat. Here are examples of unconventional breakfasts that are just as nutritious, balanced, and low in calories as cereal and milk.

- A grilled peanut butter and banana sandwich—a favorite of Elvis (but make the bread whole grain)

- Reheated cheese, vegetable, or mushroom pizza—perfect Monday or Tuesday morning fare for sports fans who indulged during a weekend game

- A turkey sandwich on whole grain bread with lettuce and tomato

- An egg salad sandwich on a whole grain English muffin— like fast food but with healthier carbs and less fat

PREPARE IN THE P.M. Mornings are a mad rush? Understood. That's still no reason to totally skip breakfast, though. The trick is to start preparing early—even the night before. To help yourself out, try any of these evening approaches.

- If you have a coffeemaker with a timer, remember to fill it and set it for the desired time. Otherwise, just fill the

Grab-and-Go Menu

Even when you're eating on the go, it's possible to have a balanced meal that includes protein, carbohydrate, and a fruit or vegetable. (You'll read much more about the importance of this balance in Step Two.) You can accomplish that with a meal-replacement drink or with these combinations of grab-and-go foods.

PROTEIN	CARBOHYDRATE	FRUIT
1 hard-boiled egg	1 small low-fat bran muffin	1 medium banana
30 g (1 oz) string cheese	1 mini-bagel	1 medium apple
2 cups low-fat milk	1 cereal bar	20 seedless grapes
1 cup low-fat yogurt	2 tablespoons box cereal	1 small box raisins
1 30-g (8-oz) bag peanuts	1 instant cereal packet	1 juice box

machine in the evening so all you have to do in the morning is turn it on.

- Hard-boil eggs and put them in the refrigerator.

- Set out plates, bowls, flatware, and nonperishable foods such as cereal and muffins so they're ready when you are.

Upstage Your Appetite

As a rule, people who eat small amounts all day long tend to chow down less when they finally have a real meal, but that's not always the case. If you still find yourself eating dinners fit for a farmer, try eating a small part of the meal—such as a slice of low-fat cheese—about 20 minutes before you sit down. That's how long it takes food to trigger "fullness" centers in the brain. The premeal snack will dial down the urge to overeat at the table.

- Do chores that you normally save until morning, such as putting out the trash, making bag lunches, or emptying the dishwasher. (This may have the added advantage of keeping you from snacking at night.)

- Cut up fruit that you can spoon into a bowl with your cereal for an instant breakfast.

- Slice bagels in half and store them in an airtight plastic bag.

Eat Between Meals

"Don't eat between meals." "Don't spoil your appetite." You've heard these bromides since you were a kid, and you may even have passed them along to your own children—but being time-worn doesn't make them true.

Before you're out the door in the morning, think ahead to when you're likely to eat again. Chances are, it won't be until past noon or 1 P.M. If you have breakfast at 7 A.M., that's more than 5 hours between meals—and that's too long. Solution: Have a light snack around midmorning. (Hint: Unless healthy foods are easy to get wherever you are during the day, you'll want to pack your snack before you leave the house.)

Why do you need a snack? It takes about 4 hours to digest a meal—5 hours, tops. At the end of 5 hours, your stomach is completely empty, and your intricately tuned metabolism is going into "uh-oh" mode. Is more food on the way? Your body has no way of knowing. You might assume that it starts tapping fat stores for fuel as a result, but what mainly happens is that it begins to slow your metabolism to conserve energy. That makes it harder to burn fat, not easier. It's a little like what happens when you let the gas gauge on your car drift down into the red zone. When you think you're running on fumes, you lighten up on the accelerator.

After lunch, the story is the same: If you won't be eating again for 5 hours or more, have something about halfway between lunch and dinner.

Some nutrition researchers estimate that spreading your calories throughout the day instead of heaping them on in big meals makes the body burn as many as 10 percent more calories. Just as important, it prevents major hunger pangs that make you want to eat everything in sight. No wonder a study conducted at the University of Massachusetts Medical Center in 2003 found that people who ate four times a day were 45 percent less likely to be obese than people who ate three times or less. Other studies support the notion that eating more often facilitates weight loss.

Curb Nighttime Noshing

Now for a final guideline: Try to eat your last meal of the day no later than 7 P.M. In a sense, mastering your timing throughout the day is all about meeting this last goal, because it helps solve a big problem that's common among people with diabetes: eating—and overeating—at night. That's when most of us have more time to sit down for a big meal. Then we turn on the tube and continue to nosh. If this describes you, you're not alone. Clinical experience suggests that most overweight people with diabetes eat more calories at night than at any other time of day.

A big shot of calories is exactly the opposite of what you really need, however. At night, your metabolism winds down as your body prepares for sleep. In terms of physiology, this is when your body needs

Right-Sizing Your Snacks

The only danger of snacks is that they can become more like added meals if you go overboard. If you're careful, though, there's no reason that between-meal eating can't be both light and satisfying. You'll do fine if you limit snacks to no more than 150 calories. Good choices that fit the bill include:

- 1 cup fat-free, sugar-free yogurt
- 30 g (1 oz) fat-free string cheese
- A plastic bag of cherry tomatoes or sliced raw red peppers, carrots, or cucumbers
- 1 medium dill pickle (if you don't need to watch your sodium intake)
- 4 cups air-popped popcorn
- 1 apple, orange, or banana

Secrets of a Successful Snacker

Linda Anthony explains her former eating patterns this way: "I was raised Italian." Growing up in her family, that meant food, and lots of it. "We ate when we were happy. We ate when we were sad. We ate when we got together. My whole upbringing revolved around food," she says. Meals, not snacks, were the focal point—and the meals were huge. "For lunch, I might have two sandwiches with thick wedges of bologna," she says. "For dinner, I'd have two or three huge helpings of spaghetti." She ate mainly at meals but would often continue eating into the night. "It's embarrassing to say, but I've been known to eat an entire pizza—eight slices—all by myself," she says.

The results of her poor eating patterns were clear to see. At 160 cm (5'3"), she weighed 109 kg (240 lb), and her blood sugar levels were up to 13 mmol/L. When it looked as if she might need medication to control her glucose, an alarm went off in her head. "My mom lost her sight, had kidney trouble, and died from complications of diabetes at age 69," she says. "It scared me straight."

She started a walking program and began cutting back on calories at meals. After a lifetime of lavish eating, though, eating less at the table was tough. That's where having small snacks between meals came in. "Timing my eating really helped me a lot," she says. "I wouldn't feel as hungry when I came to supper, so I'd eat less."

The foods Anthony chose made a difference as well. Never a big fruit eater ("My attitude was that it wouldn't stick to your ribs," she says), she keeps high-fiber produce such as bananas on hand as a staple. But she loves vegetables, too, and she carries items such as grape tomatoes wherever she goes. "I even munch on cucumbers," she says. "It may not look attractive, but you've gotta do what you've gotta do!"

Best of all, she's found creative ways to make healthy snacks seem downright sinful. One of her own recipes— "for when I need a chocolate fix"—is to make sugar-free, fat-free chocolate pudding and mix it with fat-free whipped topping to make chocolate mousse. For extra flavor, she sprinkles sugar-free gelatin powder into the mix for a chocolate-cherry or -raspberry treat. Another favorite is vanilla pudding with lime or orange gelatin powder. "It tastes just like key lime pie or a Creamsicle," she says.

Within six months, Anthony dropped 18 kg (40 lb). More amazing is her long-term progress: After sticking to the plan for 17 months, she lost 54 kg (120 lb)! No need to double-check the number—that's half her starting weight. Her blood sugar now averages 5—well into the normal range. And believe it or not, she says, "I'm not feeling deprived."

calories the least, so those you take in are more likely to be stored as fat. What's more, gorging on food late in the day makes your body work hard at digestion, hindering the quiet process of tissue repair and muscle building that takes place during sleep—which is important if you're exercising. It can also make you toss and turn in bed, disrupting your sleep and making blood sugar control even harder, as you'll see in Step Six. Last but not least, eating into the wee hours may contribute to high blood sugar when you wake up in the morning.

Does that mean you have to nosh on your fingernails and nothing else while you watch TV in the evening? If you're genuinely hungry, it's fine to have a small snack, but be sure you're not just shoveling in food out of habit or because you're bored.

A Word about Exercise

Is there a best time to exercise? The short answer is yes: anytime you can fit it into your schedule. But exercise such as walking and moderate aerobics brings down blood sugar both while you do it and for up to a day afterward. While that's the big payoff, it's also a potential hazard, especially if you take medication or insulin. The reason? Let's say you've just taken oral medication or a dose of insulin to bring your blood sugar down, and then you immediately walk for an hour. The glucose-lowering combination of the treatment and the activity could send your blood sugar crashing.

On the other hand, if you're taking insulin but don't give yourself a large enough dose, your blood sugar may actually rise too high during exercise. That's because when you're physically active, the liver pumps out more glucose, and without adequate insulin, your body will have trouble shifting glucose from your blood to working muscles. Only you and your doctor can sort this all out, but you may be able to avoid most problems by following these guidelines.

- Exercise an hour or two after eating. At that point, your blood sugar levels are elevated from food, and you'll have ample glucose to fuel your muscles. At the same time, your digestive system will have finished most of its work, so it won't deplete the energy you need for your workout.

- If you take medication, ask your doctor if you can skip it before exercising or take a lower dose; the blood sugar

A Well-Timed Day

Here's how smart meal timing can play out over the course of a typical day.

8 A.M. Breakfast: ½ to 1 cup high-fiber cereal, 1 cup fat-free milk, and 1 medium banana

9 A.M. Exercise opportunity

10:30 A.M. Snack: 20 red grapes

1 P.M. Lunch: Turkey breast on whole grain bread with mustard, 1 cup vegetable soup, 1 to 2 cups tossed salad, 1 tablespoon low-calorie salad dressing, and diet iced tea

2 P.M. Exercise opportunity

4 P.M. Snack: ¾ cup blended fat-free, sugar-free yogurt

6:30 P.M. Dinner: 115 g (4 oz) baked salmon, small baked potato with no-calorie butter-flavored spray, 1 cup steamed broccoli, ½ cup steamed carrots, and 1 cup sliced fresh strawberries with 2 tablespoons fat-free whipped topping

7:30 P.M. Exercise opportunity

10 P.M. Snack (optional): 1 cup fat-free, sugar-free chocolate pudding made with fat-free or low-fat milk

drop from physical activity may be able to substitute for the drug. Otherwise, avoid exercising when the effects of your medication peak.

- If you use insulin, time your workouts so you're not active when the effects of the insulin peak, often within the first hour or two after an injection. Your doctor will probably want you to monitor your blood sugar before and after exercise to see how activity affects it, and based on those results, he may want you to adjust your insulin dose before you exercise.

STEP 2 master the plate approach

Now you're ready to get down to the nitty-gritty—what to eat. So get a plate and set yourself a place at the table, because your plate, and how you fill it, is the main focus of the 10 Percent Plan.

In this step, you'll discover a visual approach to eating that's perfect for people with diabetes. It's called the Plate Approach, and it's amazingly simple.

The Plate Approach rebalances your meals to give you the ideal proportions of vegetables, protein, and carbohydrates. It's this perfect balance that will help you lose weight and keep your blood sugar under control. Using the Plate Approach automatically cuts your calorie intake—the real goal of any weight-loss plan. It also ensures that you won't get too many carbohydrates at one sitting, with no need for you to keep a tally. Best of all, your plate will contain plenty of food, so you'll never feel deprived.

Imagine sitting down to a typical Canadian dinner—perhaps the one you're having tonight. What do you see? If you're serving a home-style favorite, chances are that meat dominates the plate. Maybe it's a big, juicy steak tipping the scales at 225 g (80 oz) or more, enough to fill about half the plate. The rest of the plate might contain a boat-size baked potato topped with sour cream, plus maybe, crowded to one side, a few token green beans (or more likely, corn slathered with butter).

A disaster? Pretty much. This is the kind of eating that packs on weight and clogs arteries. (Remember, heart disease is a serious risk for people with diabetes.) A recent Harvard study even suggests that getting a lot of iron from red meat raises the risk of developing diabetes.

Fighting Disease while You Fight Diabetes

Many low-carb diets skimp on vegetables, and that's a shame. Vegetables are chock-full of phytochemicals, natural plant chemicals that help the body defend itself against disease and the ravages of aging. For instance, broccoli, cabbage, and other members of the cruciferous vegetable family fight cancer; tomatoes, carrots, and red peppers are packed with antioxidants and chemicals that help protect the eyes; and many vegetables contain bioflavonoids, which help neutralize unstable molecules called free radicals that can hasten aging and the development of heart disease and cancer, as well as other chemicals that stimulate the body's immune cells and infection-fighting enzymes.

Does that mean you have to give up meat and potatoes? No way. But to lose weight and bring blood sugar down, you will need to make some adjustments, mostly to the way foods are distributed on your plate. The Plate Approach will help you do this. It's a simple visual approach to making smart decisions about what to eat. The biggest change? That humble helping of vegetables will become a hearty helping, shrinking the space left over for fatty meat and starchy carbs—the major sources of calories.

How the Plate Approach Works

Use the three main elements of a typical meal—meat, starch, and vegetables—as your starting point. When you dish them out, your plate in effect becomes divided into three sections. Those three sections will be the basis of how you decide what to eat using the Plate Approach.

Of course, it's the size of the sections that matters. To picture how your plate should look when you use the Plate Approach, mentally divide it into left and right halves. Then imagine the right half split into two equal parts. Whenever you eat a meal, keep these sections in mind and fill them in the following way.

1. **LEFT SIDE: VEGETABLES.** Choose anything you like except potatoes and corn, which actually belong in the starch section. For some meals, you can eat fruit instead of (or in addition to) vegetables.

2. **TOP RIGHT: STARCHES.** This means carbohydrates such as whole grain bread or pasta, brown rice, potatoes, or corn.

3. **BOTTOM RIGHT: PROTEIN FOODS.** These include lean red meat, eggs, fish, chicken, and turkey, as well as dairy products, such as yogurt or cheese.

A Plate Makeover

Using the Plate Approach, the number of calories you save by emphasizing vegetables instead of fatty foods can be significant.

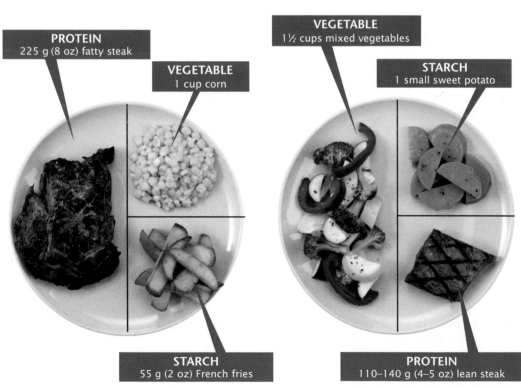

1,058 CALORIES

PROTEIN
225 g (8 oz) fatty steak

VEGETABLE
1 cup corn

STARCH
55 g (2 oz) French fries

440 CALORIES

VEGETABLE
1½ cups mixed vegetables

STARCH
1 small sweet potato

PROTEIN
110–140 g (4–5 oz) lean steak

That, in a nutshell, is the Plate Approach. At each meal, feel free to add a small amount of oil or tub margarine. (Always choose tub margarine over stick margarine to limit trans fats, those "partially hydrogenated" oils that raise LDL, or "bad" cholesterol, and clog arteries.) Now eat everything—no need to hold back. In fact, you can fill the biggest portion of your plate—the vegetable section—again and again if you're still hungry. That's right, there's *no limit* on the amount of food you can eat from this part of the plate as long as you stop when you feel satisfied. On the right half of the plate, however, stick with one helping of carbohydrate and protein.

Beans: Crossover Calories

What do you do with legumes (starchy beans), which cross the line between carbohydrate and protein? Answer: Just about anything. The foods in question—such as kidney, navy, and lima beans and even baked beans—are technically vegetables, but they're packed with plant protein as well as carbohydrates. Because beans are higher in calories than nonstarchy vegetables, you shouldn't eat unlimited amounts, so they don't belong on the vegetable half of your plate. Instead, use them as either a starch or a protein. For example, if you're making chili, use kidney beans in place of meat to save fat and calories. Or if you want chicken and baked beans for dinner, think of the beans as your starch.

Why is the Plate Approach so effective? Partly because it's so intuitive. There are no carbohydrates, or even calories, to count. You don't have to look up any food exchanges or consult the glycemic index. And unlike some low-carb diets, it doesn't require you to practically cut out entire food groups. If you find that these other methods work, more power to you—but studies suggest that simpler approaches work just as well while being easier to stick with over the long term. And of course, it's the long term that counts.

Besides being easy to follow, the Plate Approach has three distinct advantages: It cuts calories, controls carbs, and satisfies your hunger.

BENEFIT 1 THE PLATE APPROACH CUTS CALORIES

There's no escaping it: To lose weight, you need to take in fewer calories than you burn. The Plate Approach's solution to cutting calories is remarkably simple: Eat more vegetables and less of everything else. In the Plate Approach, half the real estate on your plate is taken up by vegetables, which are naturally very low in calories, so there's less room for starches and calorie-dense meats.

Vegetables are low in calories yet high in volume because a lot of their weight comes from water. Such "high-volume" foods have the advantage of looking big, so they make your brain expect that you'll be satisfied by eating them. They also take up more room in your stomach, so they trigger a signal in your brain that makes you stop eating sooner.

By eating more vegetables, you'll automatically eat less fat—and that's important, since fat has more than twice the calories of carbohydrates or protein. The calorie differences can be dramatic. Just look at how the calories in a small amount of cheese compare with those in a smorgasbord of vegetables (below). It's small wonder that researchers in weight-loss programs throughout North America find that when people eat lots of vegetables, their calorie consumption goes down—and they lose weight.

All About Calories

For about the same calories you'd get in two small pieces of cheese, you could fill up on a mountain of vegetables.

225 CALORIES

220 CALORIES

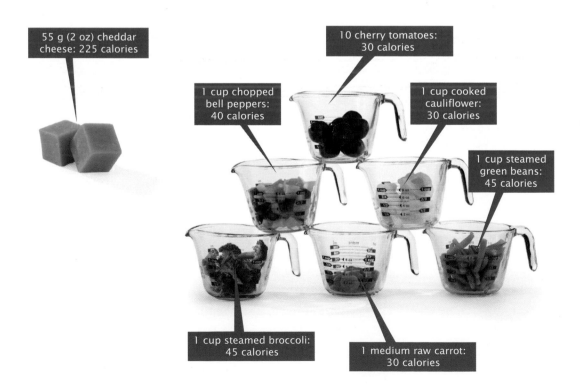

55 g (2 oz) cheddar cheese: 225 calories

10 cherry tomatoes: 30 calories

1 cup chopped bell peppers: 40 calories

1 cup cooked cauliflower: 30 calories

1 cup steamed green beans: 45 calories

1 cup steamed broccoli: 45 calories

1 medium raw carrot: 30 calories

quiz
Making Choices, Making Changes

Succeeding with an eating plan is a combination of habit and knowledge. To get a handle on how close your current eating habits are to the Plate Approach, circle the numbers next to the answers that best reflect your decisions and attitudes.

1. **What's the star of most of your lunches and dinners?**
   1 Meat
   2 Starch (pasta, potatoes, bread, rice, or corn)
   3 Vegetables (except potatoes or corn)

2. **Not counting potatoes and corn, how much room do vegetables usually occupy on your plate?**
   1 No room—I eat only potatoes and corn
   2 About a quarter of the plate
   3 Half of the plate or more

3. **What is your usual choice when eating bread?**
   1 White bread
   2 Wheat bread
   3 Whole wheat or other whole grain bread

4. **Circle all that apply:**
   1 I tend to eat the same few vegetables all the time
   2 Vegetables are boring
   3 I would eat more vegetables if I knew how to cook them

5. **How often do you eat salads?**
   1 Only when I go to a restaurant
   2 Salads are boring, so I rarely eat them
   3 I have a salad with my meals several times per week

6. **Which of these fats do you think are good for you?**
   1 The fats in meat or full-fat dairy products
   2 Butter, margarine, or vegetable shortening
   3 Olive oil, canola oil, or peanut butter

7. **How often do you have a low-fat dairy product, such as low-fat or fat-free milk, cheese, or yogurt?**
   1 Rarely or never
   2 Once a day
   3 Two or three times a day

8. **On average, how many soft drinks do you have each day?**
   1 Three or more
   2 One or two
   3 None

Tally your score, then turn the page.

quiz
What Your Score Means

20 to 24: You should have no trouble adjusting to the Plate Approach because you're already applying many of the concepts behind it.

14 to 19: You're on your way to following the Plate Approach, but you'll need to make a few adjustments. Look at the questions you scored with a 3 and ask yourself why these healthy habits seem easier to you than those you scored lower—there may be lessons you can apply to areas where you need to do more work.

8 to 13: You'll need to start making changes a little at a time to get closer to the Plate Approach. By eating more vegetables and smaller portions of other foods, you'll see significant effects on your waistline and blood sugar. Place checkmarks next to questions you answered with a 1 to get a handle on the changes you need to emphasize first.

The logic behind the questions:

1. If you answered "vegetables," you're well on your way to success with the 10 Percent Plan. Nothing delivers more nutrients with fewer calories. And you can eat vegetables to your heart's content without worrying about gaining weight. If you answered "meat" or "starch," this chapter will show you how to rethink the space protein and carbohydrate foods occupy on your plate. These foods aren't off-limits, but adjusting the balance will almost guarantee that you'll lose weight and bring your blood sugar down.

2. For many Canadians, potatoes and corn occupy larger portions of the plate than they should. Giving other, non-starchy vegetables a more dominant place on your plate is a sure way to lose weight.

3. If you checked number 3, good for you! Whole grain bread has less impact on blood sugar than white. "Wheat" bread is not the same as "whole wheat" bread.

4. If you checked any of these, you're probably stuck in a vegetable rut. It's time to discover new ways to get more vegetables into your diet.

5. Salads are a perfect way to add vegetables to meals, but if you eat them in restaurants, ask for the dressing on the side. Prewashed lettuce and precut vegetables have made salad prep a snap. If you think salads are boring, turn to page 71 for fun toppings.

6. Olive and canola oil consist mostly of healthy fats, the kinds that help stave off heart disease. All the others contribute to heart disease.

7. You'll want to have dairy two or three times a day on the 10 Percent Plan, not only because it's a good source of protein but also because most products made from milk contain calcium, which can help you lose weight.

8. Soft drinks add calories without filling you up the way solid foods do. Diet soft drinks are okay, but try not to overdo them, since they tend to stimulate your sweet tooth. Water is the best choice.

BENEFIT 2 THE PLATE APPROACH CONTROLS CARBS

Contrary to popular belief, carbohydrates aren't dietary villains, even if you have diabetes. Rather, they're the body's main source of energy. They are a major provider of B vitamins, iron, and fiber, as well as the trace mineral chromium, which is thought to help cells use insulin. Carbohydrates are also protein sparing, which means that the body uses them first for energy and leaves protein to be used for body repair and other important functions. Thus, you obviously don't want to cut them out of your diet.

At the same time, you don't want to get too many carbohydrates at one sitting, because carbs break down into glucose more easily than fat or protein. A big bowl of spaghetti can really make your blood sugar soar. The Plate Approach helps you get the right balance by asking you to confine starches to one-quarter of your plate.

The Great Carb Debate

Chances are, you're confused about carbohydrates. It's become fashionable to think you shouldn't eat them, yet they're an essential part of a balanced diet. What's the real deal?

Carbs (the kinds in sugary foods and starches) are sometimes blamed for contributing to the obesity epidemic. And while it's true that eating too many of them—or any other type of food—leads to weight gain, there's more to it than that. Some researchers now believe that carbohydrates make weight control especially hard for people who are already too heavy. The reason: Carbs break down easily into glucose, and with enough glucose on hand, the body never has to burn its fat stores for energy.

So doesn't it make sense to shun carbs? Possibly, but you shouldn't avoid them altogether. First, carbohydrates such as whole grains are important sources of fiber, vitamins, and minerals. Several studies have actually suggested that eating whole grains lowers the risk of diabetes, not to mention heart disease and stroke.

Second, it's still total calories that count most, no matter where those calories come from. Consider the results of one recent study that tested two dramatically different diets—one low in carbs and the other low in fat. Despite their opposite approaches, the diets had one thing in common: Both were low in calories. The result? After six weeks, people on both diets lost about the same amount of weight.

The Plate Approach limits both fat and carbs, but just as important as limiting carbs is choosing the right ones—the "slow-burning" type known as complex carbohydrates. We'll help you do that.

BENEFIT 3 THE PLATE APPROACH KEEPS HUNGER IN CHECK

Making sure you get protein at every meal is critical because protein makes you feel full longer than carbohydrates do. That's remarkable because protein has the same number of calories (4 per gram) as carbs. Protein also has the advantage of being digested more slowly than carbohydrates, so it doesn't have the dramatic impact on blood sugar that carbs do. Beyond these advantages, your body needs protein to build everything from muscles to hardworking enzymes, immune system cells, and hormones.

If protein is so great, shouldn't you eat a high-protein diet to lose weight even faster? No. One reason not to go overboard on protein is that the high-protein foods we eat most often—especially meat—also tend to be high in saturated fat. That's the type of fat people with diabetes need like a hole in the head, since it clogs arteries that are already vulnerable to heart disease and makes cells more resistant to insulin (the real problem behind type 2 diabetes).

Another reason is that filling up on protein would mean eating fewer carbohydrates, the body's primary source of fuel. That would be like ripping the lumber out of the walls of your house to feed your furnace instead of using gas or oil. Protein

Fiber: A Side Benefit

An extra benefit of the Plate Approach is that with all the vegetables and complex carbohydrates you'll eat, you'll get plenty of fiber. Fiber may not be sexy as far as nutrients go—in fact, technically, it's not even considered a nutrient, since your body can't digest it—but it's important for several reasons.

▸ It slows digestion and keeps blood sugar from rising quickly after a meal. This effect is so powerful that it can lower your overall blood sugar levels. Because it slows digestion, fiber also keeps you feeling full longer.

▸ It adds bulk to food, so it makes you feel full without adding calories. One study found that over the course of 10 years, people who ate a lot of high-fiber foods weighed an average of 4.5 kg (10 lb) less than people who ate little fiber.

▸ Soluble fiber, found in foods such as beans, barley, and oatmeal, can cut your cholesterol and lower your risk of heart disease.

▸ A high-fiber diet keeps you "regular," making problems such as constipation, spastic colon, and hemorrhoids (common in people with type 2 diabetes) less likely. It may also cut your risk of colon cancer.

doesn't burn as efficiently as carbohydrate or fat. In fact, to be used as fuel, it must undergo chemical changes that release toxic by-products. The body flushes out these toxins in urine, which helps explain why high-protein diets can make you lose weight fast: They cause water loss. When you start eating normally again, the weight comes back.

High-protein diets may even endanger your health by overworking your kidneys—and people with diabetes already have an elevated risk of kidney damage.

Using the Plate Approach

Now it's time to put the Plate Approach to work. The first step: Make sure your plate is the right size. No, we're not going to ask you to eat dinner from a salad plate. Remember, the meals you eat on the Plate Approach are supposed to be generous and satisfying! That means you'll be filling up a standard-size plate, which should have 20 to 23 cm (8 to 9 in.) of eating surface. It's okay if the lip of the plate makes the dimensions bigger than that: You're only concerned with the area that you actually fill with food. For a ready-made, preportioned dish that can help you use the Plate Approach, try using a segmented plate such as those that parents use to serve children. Some heavy-duty paper plates are also divided into three sections of just about the right size.

Not every meal will fit precisely into different segments of a plate the way we've suggested. For example, a stir-fry might have all the right elements—carbs (brown rice), lean protein (chicken strips), and lots of vegetables (carrots, broccoli, and pea pods)—but the ingredients are mixed together. That's okay. Once you have the basic idea of the Plate Approach and get used to seeing how much food goes into each section of the plate, you won't need the divisions to guide you. As long as the bulk of the dish is vegetables, with smaller amounts of rice and poultry, a stir-fry is a perfect Plate Approach meal.

A word about breakfast: We're not going to ask you to fill half your plate with vegetables at this meal, since most of us don't eat vegetables in the morning (although if you're making an omelet, go ahead and pack it with as much produce as possible). Instead, substitute fruit, such as blueberries, strawberries, or bananas—or orange juice—for vegetables.

In Step Three, we'll show you options for every meal so you can see how easy it is to make the Plate Approach work over the course of a week.

Filling the Vegetable Side of the Plate

Almost all vegetables are on the approved list for unlimited eating with the Plate Approach. The exceptions are potatoes, corn, and legumes such as lima beans, which belong in the smaller starch section of your plate (you're limited to one serving of these). Why? These starchy vegetables are higher in calories than other vegetables.

We have a tendency to lump all vegetables together as if they were a single food. But vegetables can be sweet, bitter, or bland; big or small; and green, orange, yellow, red, brown, and every shade in between. Given the sheer bounty of natural foods at your disposal, how do you decide which to eat?

The first thing to do is to vote with your taste buds and eat produce you like. If you tend to eat only one veggie, such as green beans, though, try to vary your routine. This will help ensure that you get all the nutrients you need. A serving of broccoli may have dozens of powerhouse nutrients—but not necessarily the same ones as a serving of asparagus. You may even gain a bonus in the weight-loss battle by varying your veggies: Studies suggest that people who eat a variety of foods, especially vegetables,

Help!

My family hates vegetables—and I'm not willing to make separate meals. How do I fight this?

The first thing to do is explore why they don't like vegetables. The problem could be a simple matter of preparation. If you've always cooked vegetables, maybe your family would like them better raw—or vice-versa. It's a common error to cook vegetables to death, making them mushy and bland. Instead, try lightly steaming vegetables such as cauliflower so they're appealingly hot but still have a gratifying crunch. Or maybe your family would be more open to veggies if they were incorporated into casseroles or stir-fries rather than served as a side dish.

Also, don't assume that past dislikes are set in stone: Tastes change with age, and you may be surprised to find that family members will now eat foods they once wouldn't touch. What's more, studies find that exposing people to a food more frequently makes them likelier to accept it. So keep trying! And don't forget: You have diabetes, and good food is good medicine. Maybe your family members are the ones who need to adapt.

tend to consume less fat and are less likely to be overweight than people stuck in dietary ruts.

Start by first choosing veggies with star nutritional power. As a rule of thumb, vivid colors—dark greens and bright reds or yellows—signal that a vegetable is packed with vitamins, minerals, and other vital nutrients. You can't go wrong with the following favorites.

Asparagus

Just 1 cup of asparagus packs a whopping 4 grams of fiber. It also has plenty of B vitamins, vitamin C, and folate.

TIP: Use asparagus spears within two days of purchase because they lose their vitamin C quickly. Steam the spears and then sprinkle with lemon juice or ginger-flavored soy sauce for extra flavor. Or try roasting them in the oven with a little olive oil. Delicious! Make instant asparagus soup by

Vegetables As Volumizers

Vegetables add volume to your meals without adding a lot of calories. Bulking up dishes such as pasta with vegetables instead of high-fat sauce allows you to eat significantly more for the same number of calories.

380 CALORIES   380 CALORIES

1 cup cooked fettuccine

½ cup Alfredo sauce

2 teaspoons olive oil
2 teaspoons Parmesan cheese

1 cup cooked fettuccine

3 cups steamed vegetables

pureeing cooked asparagus, heating it with a little milk, and adding chopped parsley or tarragon.

Bell peppers

Whether red, yellow, or green, peppers are full of B vitamins and vitamin C. Red peppers also contain beta-carotene, which the body converts to vitamin A, a nutrient that helps protect the eyes.

TIP: With their large lobes and airy interiors, peppers are perfect for stuffing, but you'll need to clean out the seeds, which can be bitter. To do it, use a sharp knife to cut a circle around the stem, then lift it out, along with the interior membranes that hold the seeds. Rinse the inside of the pepper to wash out any stragglers.

Broccoli

This cruciferous vegetable is often touted as the king of vegetables. It's loaded with vitamins A and C as well as other antioxidants (compounds that help guard against cancer and heart disease, among other things), and it even contains calcium, which may help lower high blood pressure (common in people with type 2 diabetes).

TIP: Overcooking can degrade some of broccoli's nutrients, so steam florets lightly, shorten cooking time in the microwave, or quickly stir-fry them in a small amount of olive oil. To eat them almost raw but cooked enough to soften them up, blanch broccoli spears in boiling water for about 3 minutes.

Vegetable Seasoning Guide

Asparagus	Lemon, garlic, oregano
Broccoli	Garlic, soy sauce, mustard, dark sesame oil
Carrots	Lemon, orange, curry powder, ginger, dill, raspberry vinegar
Cauliflower	Basil, curry powder
Eggplant	Basil, garlic, crushed tomato
Green beans	Garlic, soy sauce, sesame seeds
Mushrooms	Parsley, thyme, green onions, chives, sherry, balsamic vinegar
Peas	Mint, garlic
Spinach	Garlic, soy sauce, sea salt, nutmeg, balsamic vinegar
Summer squash	Lemon, rosemary, tomato, garlic, basil
Tomato	Basil, garlic, oregano, balsamic vinegar, Parmesan cheese

Brussels sprouts

These little cabbage-like nodes are rich in vitamin C. They're also an excellent source of lutein, an antioxidant that may reduce the risk of developing cataracts—a serious concern when you're already at increased risk of eye damage due to diabetes.

TIP: The stems are tougher than the leaves, so cut an "X" across the base of each sprout before steaming to allow heat inside the core to soften it. The sprouts will cook evenly for consistent tenderness. For the mildest taste, choose frozen baby brussels sprouts. For the best flavor, cook them lightly so they're still a little crisp.

Cauliflower

The dense florets of a cauliflower head are great sources of B vitamins, which help the body metabolize glucose.

TIP: Some recipes call for serving a head of cooked cauliflower intact, but when it's broken or cut into florets, it will heat faster, so more nutrients are preserved. Faster cooking also holds back cauliflower's pungent odor, which intensifies the longer you heat it.

Dark, leafy greens

Greens such as spinach, Swiss chard, bok choy, collards, and mustard greens are some of the few plant sources of zinc, a mineral that protects insulin-producing beta cells in the pancreas. Zinc is lost in the urine when blood sugar is too high. These greens are also rich sources of calcium and magnesium—minerals that have been shown to decrease the risk of diabetes—not to mention antioxidants that protect your eyes and your heart.

Instant Vegetables 5 Easy Ways

Getting more vegetables into your diet doesn't have to involve a lot of time-consuming preparation, especially if you start with these five "convenience" foods.

Canned tomatoes. They're endlessly useful in sauces and casseroles, not to mention chili.

Frozen stir-fry vegetables. Dump them into pasta, stir-fries, casseroles, or soup, or microwave and top with low-fat shredded cheese.

Frozen spinach. Add it to cheese pizza, pasta sauce, or omelets; use in crustless quiches.

Prewashed lettuce. Use it as the base for a super-fast lunch or light meal by adding beans, vegetables, canned tuna—anything you want. Add it to sandwiches.

Veggie burger. Using a little cooking spray, fry it fast on the stove or broil in a toaster oven, then top with your favorite condiments, such as tomato, onion, and mustard.

TIP: Spinach leaves tend to attract grit. Before cooking or serving, place them in a bowl of cool water or in the sink. Swish them gently to remove the grit, then drain and repeat if necessary. To dry the leaves, give them a whirl in a salad spinner.

IT'S ALL IN THE PREPARATION

Almost all vegetables are inherently good for you, but beware of transforming low-calorie vegetables into high-calorie ones by frying them in oil or smothering them with toppings, such as cheese sauces, full-fat salad dressings, or butter. By adding just 1 teaspoon of butter, you more than double or triple the calories in a serving of vegetables.

Does this mean you have to suffer through dinners of bland and tasteless rabbit food? Hardly. There are plenty of ways to give vegetables delicious flavor without adding excess calories.

ROAST. Roasting vegetables brings out delicious sweetness. Eggplant, onions, red peppers, zucchini, portobello mushrooms, and carrots are all perfect candidates. Just slice, brush with a little olive oil or Italian dressing, and roast at 200˚C (400˚F) until done.

SEASON. Think beyond butter when it comes to seasoning vegetables. Try lemon juice, lemon-pepper seasoning, garlic salt, Mrs. Dash (a seasoning blend), or herbs. Balsamic or white vinegar also gives an appealing tang to spinach and other greens.

TOP. Add low-fat grated cheese or Parmesan, toasted almond slices, sesame seeds, or walnuts.

TAKE A LOW-EFFORT APPROACH

It's a question worth asking: Why aren't vegetables a more normal part of the Canadian diet, as they are in some other countries? One answer may be that preparing vegetables can seem like a big production, but vegetables don't always have to be served as sensational side dishes or entrées—or even as solo servings. Here are nine simple ways to sneak vegetables into meals or boost their plate appeal.

1. Stock your pantry with canned and frozen vegetables. They can be as nutritious as fresh veggies because they're picked at their peak, when they are the most nutrient-rich. Frozen

vegetables are flash-frozen, which seals in the nutrients until the veggies are thawed. Don't worry about losing nutrients that leach into water in cans: The amounts are small, and you lose nothing if you use the water in dishes such as soup.

2. Add some canned or frozen vegetables, such as carrots, peas, chopped spinach, or beans, to every soup you make.

3. Dress up a cheese pizza with mushrooms, peppers, spinach, and broccoli.

4. For an instant, perfectly dressed salad, open a bag of prewashed, precut romaine lettuce or mixed greens, add a tablespoon of olive oil and a splash of lemon juice or balsamic vinegar, and shake.

5. Keep your kitchen stocked with vegetables that keep well, such as carrots, celery, onions, cucumbers, squash, and garlic. That way, you'll always have produce on hand even when it's tough to get to the store for more perishable items.

6. To save time, buy precut vegetables.

7. Put raw vegetables out on a plate while you're making dinner so you can snack on them instead of higher-calorie temptations such as chips or other starchy foods. Find a low-fat vegetable dip the whole family enjoys to go with the crudités.

8. Lightly steam vegetables in a stovetop or microwave steamer for 3 to 5 minutes, until the color turns brighter (this is the point at which they're most nutritious). Then eat the crisp-tender vegetables either hot with the meal or cold as a snack.

9. Add frozen stir-fry vegetables to canned chicken broth and heat for about 5 minutes for a quick, nutritious soup. Add soy sauce or miso paste for an Asian flavor.

Making Salads Interesting

Plain lettuce salads are boring—no wonder some people think they don't like salad! To add more appeal, vary the greens, and choose two or three of these items as toppings.

- Almonds
- Artichoke hearts
- Baby corn
- Chickpeas
- Craisins
- Flaxseed
- Grapefruit sections
- Hearts of palm
- Kidney beans
- Mandarin orange wedges
- Mango slices
- Olives
- Peanuts
- Pecans
- Raspberries
- Red grapes
- Starfruit slices
- Strawberry slices
- Sunflower seeds
- Walnuts
- Water chestnuts

LEARNING TO LIKE VEGETABLES

What if you just don't love the taste of vegetables? If that's the case, it's probably because you simply aren't used to eating them. People who think they don't like vegetables can actually end up loving them if they introduce them gradually, which gives the palate a chance to develop a taste for them. The following strategies will also help.

- Try preparing vegetables in different ways, since texture, not taste, may be the problem. Cooking them a little less or more than usual will change the texture and perhaps even the taste. You may also find that you like some veggies better raw than cooked.

- Serve "baby" versions of vegetables such as carrots, green beans, and brussels sprouts, which tend to have more appealing texture and slightly sweeter flavor.

- Get your vegetables in disguise—for example, in vegetable juice or salsa, which contains onions, peppers, and tomatoes. Use salsa as a dip for vegetables or a topping for baked potatoes.

- Add chopped or pureed carrots to meat loaf; this disguises the vegetable without substantially changing the taste of the meat. Similarly, put chopped or pureed spinach (or anything else that appeals to you) in lasagna, bread dough, or pasta sauce.

FRUIT: NOT TO BE FORGOTTEN

So far, we've been talking mostly about vegetables, but fruit deserves a place on your plate, too. Surprised? Don't be. Some people believe that the sugar in fruit makes it off-limits for people with diabetes, but that isn't the case. Fructose—fruit sugar—isn't absorbed as quickly as the sucrose in table sugar and sweets (thanks in large part to fruit's fiber), so it won't send your blood sugar soaring as high. Just as important, fruits have almost all the advantages that vegetables do— they're brimming with nutrients you need, they're low in fat, they're high in fiber, and they're relatively low in calories compared with many other foods.

At the same time, you can't eat fruit with abandon, because fructose makes it higher in calories than most veggies. How much can you eat? Aim to get three or four servings a day. (A serving is one piece of whole fruit, ½ cup of cooked or canned fruit, or 1 cup of raw fruit.) Some approaches to consider:

- Have one piece of fruit with each meal: berries or melon at breakfast, an apple or banana at lunch, and a fruit-based dessert after dinner.

- Eat fruit at breakfast, then as a snack at midmorning and midafternoon.

- Reserve fruit entirely for snacks at midmorning, midafternoon, and bedtime.

As with vegetables, it's a good idea to vary the kinds of fruits you eat every day, since different fruits provide different nutrients.

A final point: Strive to make most of your fruit servings real produce, not juice. Many of the nutrients and a lot of the fiber found in the skin, flesh, and seeds of fruit are eliminated during juicing, and the calories are concentrated in juice, so you get more than you would if you ate the fruit. For example, 1 cup of orange sections has 85 calories, while a cup of orange juice from frozen concentrate has 110, a difference of 25 calories. That may not sound like much, but small differences like these can quickly add up. An extra 25 calories a day can mean a gain of more than 1 kg (2 lb) a year. What's more, drinking juice doesn't give you the gratifying effort of chewing, so it's easy to suck down calories without feeling satisfied.

The Carb Quarter

When we told you to fill a quarter of your plate with carbohydrates, chances are you didn't say "Great! I'll fill it with jelly beans, cupcakes, snack crackers, or cookies!" even though you could have, because those are all carbohydrates. But does that mean that sweets are as good for you as other carbs, such as brown rice? Of course not. Sugary foods contribute little in the way of nutrition but plenty of calories. And that's not the only issue at hand.

Here's the real reason that not all carbs are created equal, especially for people with diabetes. "Simple" or "refined" carbs, such as table sugar, white bread, cereals made primarily from rice or corn, and most baked goods and snack foods, are digested quickly. In no time, they're broken down into glucose, which sends your blood sugar soaring. In turn, your body pumps out more insulin to handle the sudden flood of glucose, and when all that insulin kicks in, blood sugar plummets, leaving you shaky and hungry again in no time. Needless to say, these are not the carbs we want you to focus on.

HAIL THE WHOLE, REFUSE THE REFINED

The foods that should occupy the quarter of your plate dedicated to carbohydrates are "complex" carbs. They are, in essence, grains that have not been stripped of their fiber and nutrients. These "whole" grains take longer to digest and therefore won't raise your blood sugar as dramatically as processed carbohydrates do. They also contain far more vitamins and minerals than refined carbs.

Many Canadians aren't used to eating whole grains and may not know where to begin. Fortunately, it's not difficult to do.

- Buy bread and rolls with the word *whole* on the label, and the name of the grain as the first ingredient. This is the easiest way to shift the balance from simple to complex carbs in your diet. Don't be fooled by words that manufacturers sometimes use to make their products sound healthier than they are. For example, coloring a loaf of bread brown and calling it wheat bread doesn't make it whole wheat. Or saying a product is "made with wheat flour" could be true of both whole wheat bread and angel food cake. If a product is truly whole grain, the label will list whole wheat, whole oats, or some other whole grain as the first ingredient on the label.

- Eat a breakfast of champions. Some of the most accessible (and tasty) sources of whole grains can be found in your breakfast bowl, in cereals such as oatmeal, Grape-Nuts,

5 Things to Do with a Bag of Barley

Barley is one of the richest sources of cholesterol-lowering soluble fiber, but people don't often think to include it in their diets—and maybe you aren't sure how. Here are some ideas to get you started.

1. Add it to soups and stews as a more nutritious alternative to pasta or noodles.
2. Make a side dish by sautéing vegetables such as onions, garlic, and carrots, then adding barley and herbs, such as sage and thyme, and simmering in water according to the package directions.
3. Try a barley salad topped with a sprinkling of Parmesan cheese.
4. Add barley to chili as a textured thickener that will allow you to use less meat.
5. Use it in place of rice to stuff bell peppers.

The Fast Track

Want to lower your blood sugar faster? Watch what you drink. Some beverages pack on the weight, while others can actually help moderate glucose swings—as can a certain spice we encourage you to cook with.

Take Aim at Sodas

These beverages have zero nutritional value, but each 355 ml (12-oz) serving of regular soda contains about 150 calories—virtually all of it sugar. (That's equivalent to nine packets of sugar!) Studies show that soda calories don't fill you up the way food does, so you end up consuming more calories throughout the day than you would if you got those calories from something solid.

If you usually drink three cans of soda a day—not unusual if you drink soda more out of habit or convenience than desire—you can easily cut an impressive 450 calories by switching to another beverage, such as:

- Water. It has zero calories and quenches thirst better than sugary drinks. If you drink bottled water, though, beware of flavored brands, which can have as many calories as soft drinks. Check the label.

- Diet drinks with noncaloric sweeteners.

- Sparkling water. Choose plain water or sugar-free, fruit-flavored varieties.

- Iced tea. Make your own by steeping two tea bags in a tall glass of cold water. If you drink bottled iced tea, check to be sure it's sugar-free and calorie-free.

- Lemonade. Making your own with fresh lemon juice and sweetening it with a sugar substitute cuts out the calories, saving more than 100 calories compared with store-bought lemonade.

Enjoy a Cup of Joe

Love your morning coffee? Go ahead and pour a cup: Numerous studies have shown the antidiabetic effects of coffee. Recently, scientists discovered that it's not the caffeine in coffee that lowers blood sugar but other compounds, most likely ones called chlorogenic acids. In fact, you're better off drinking decaf, since caffeine hampers insulin's ability to draw glucose out of blood.

Not a coffee drinker? Try green tea. Compounds called polyphenols in green tea also appear to do battle with diabetes. In one recent study, cells from diabetic rats that drank green tea soaked up twice as much blood sugar as cells from rats that drank plain water. Black tea did not have any effect on blood sugar absorption.

Spice It Up

Add a dash of cinnamon to foods whenever you get a chance. What's special about cinnamon? Recent research finds that the spice lowers blood sugar by boosting the activity of insulin. As little as ½ teaspoon a day can lower blood sugar by as much as 29 percent.

Use cinnamon to flavor chicken stew or sprinkle it on toast, low-fat pudding, or baked apples. Add it to apple pie (you'll find a low-fat recipe on page 125). Or brew up a pot of cinnamon tea. To do it, boil 4 cups of water, add four cinnamon sticks, and simmer for 20 minutes. Strain before drinking.

and Wheat Chex. Look for a cereal that contains at least 3 g of fiber per serving—the higher the fiber content, the better.

- Give a boost to homemade baked goods by replacing one-third of the white flour with whole wheat flour.

- Use whole wheat pasta. It's becoming more widely available, along with whole wheat couscous, bulgur, and other whole grain products.

- Switch to brown rice. It may take a little while to get used to it if you usually eat white rice, but soon you'll find yourself enjoying its somewhat nutty taste and slightly crunchy texture.

Help!

I'm addicted to carbs!

Some people have a strong urge to eat—and often overeat—pasta and bread as well as sweets such as cookies and chocolate. Don't blame yourself for lack of willpower, though: There may in fact be a physical reason you crave starches. They raise blood levels of the amino acid tryptophan, which increases production of the feel-good hormone serotonin. Some experts contend that people who crave carbohydrates actually have a faulty serotonin feedback mechanism. Whether it's true or not, you're not a slave to brain chemistry. Here are some ways to calm your cravings.

- Fix the mood, not the food. Going outside for some fresh air, visiting a friend, holding a baby, playing with a pet, exercising, or enjoying a hobby can all distract you, lift your mood, keep you out of the kitchen, and possibly chase cravings away.

- Control the damage. If chocolate is your weakness, keep it in the freezer: It's tougher to wolf down when it's frozen solid. Better yet, don't keep it in the house.

- Fight food with food. When you're driven to eat salty carbs, try getting more calcium from dairy foods or other sources. Studies have found that people with low intakes of this mineral are more prone to salt cravings.

- Give yourself a "fix" of your trigger food every day. If you deny yourself altogether, you may just end up wanting the food more. Eating a moderate amount daily should stave off cravings.

- For some people, cutting out sugary foods such as chocolate and cookies altogether for two weeks makes the cravings for those foods virtually disappear. Try it!

- Food cravings sometimes indicate a need for fluids. Drink a large glass of water, then wait 10 minutes or so and see if the craving passes.

BE SMART ABOUT SWEETS

Do sweets have a place on your plate when you have diabetes? The answer is a qualified yes: There's room for any food on your plate as long as you keep calories under control. Forget the old notion that sugar is inherently bad for you. Sugar is just another form of carbohydrate, and studies over the years have led many health professionals to conclude that sugar itself doesn't make blood sugar rise any faster than any other type of carbohydrate does. However, sugary snacks and desserts can raise blood sugar faster than other foods because they contain practically no fiber—and fiber slows digestion of food and thereby tames its impact on blood sugar.

The real problem with sugar is that it has loads of calories but little nutrition. To sidestep extra calories while still indulging your sweet tooth, use sugar substitutes whenever possible. Although the safety of artificial sweeteners has been questioned over the years, numerous studies have shown them to be safe in the quantities normally used in food. There are more sugar substitutes on the market now than ever before, so you have several choices.

ASPARTAME. Sold under brand names such as NutraSweet and Equal, aspartame is 200 times sweeter than sugar. It's used as a tabletop sweetener and is generally used in foods or drinks that aren't cooked, because it can break down and lose its sweetness when heated.

ACESULFAME-K. About as sweet as aspartame but stable when heated, acesulfame-K (Sunette) is typically used in sweet foods that you cook, such as gelatins and puddings. It's also used in beverages and chewing gum and as a tabletop sweetener.

SACCHARIN. Sold as Sweet'N Low or Hermesetas, saccharin is one of the oldest sweeteners on the market. About 300 times sweeter than sugar, it has a slightly bitter aftertaste. It is allowed as an additive in the United States, but only as a tabletop sweetener in Canada.

SUCRALOSE. Although made from sugar, sucralose (Splenda) is chemically altered so the body doesn't recognize it as a carbohydrate and doesn't absorb it. It's used in a variety of low-calorie foods and drinks and as a tabletop sweetener. And it's heat stable, so you can cook with it.

Picking the Right Protein

How to fill the protein corner of your plate? Unless you're a vegetarian (vegetables such as kidney beans, lima beans, and lentils do contain protein), your answer is probably "with meat!" And meat is fine on the 10 Percent Plan—as long as you choose carefully.

Meat contains fat, and that's its downfall, because fat means calories. We're not asking you to cut all the fat from your diet—that would be crazy. Fat adds flavor, richness, and texture to foods. It makes you feel full and satisfied. And it helps the body absorb fat-soluble vitamins such as vitamins D and E. In fact, people who cut too much fat from their diets are less likely to succeed at losing weight. That doesn't mean, though, that you can eat all the fat you want or that every type of fat is good for you. In Step Three, we'll show you how you can put together meals that serve up excellent sources of protein based on the following guidelines.

CUT BACK ON SATURATED FAT

If you think fatty steaks and plates of cheese are the answer to diabetes and overweight, forget it. The culprit in most heart problems blamed on fat intake is saturated fat, found in meat and full-fat dairy products, such as cheese. Saturated fat raises "bad" LDL cholesterol, the kind that clogs blood vessels and can lead to heart attacks and strokes—risks that loom especially large when you have diabetes. Just as important for you, research shows that saturated fat may increase insulin resistance and make blood sugar control more difficult.

5 Things to Do with a Can of Beans

First, drain and rinse the beans, then:

1. Add chickpeas or kidney beans to a salad for a filling fix of protein.
2. Pour canned beans into soup or chili.
3. Add some to pasta sauce for an Italian-style dish.
4. Make a tasty black-bean salad (See recipe on page 224.)
5. Mash kidney beans or black beans and use them on tortillas instead of refried beans.

The trick, then, is to choose lean meats and low-fat dairy products. Simple enough, right? In the next chapter, you'll find plenty of meals that fit the bill. Even some of your favorite "bad-for-you" foods—such as burgers, macaroni and cheese, and fried chicken—get the lower-fat treatment in the recipes beginning on page 106.

In general, you want to:

- Choose meats that are relatively low in saturated fat. "Select" is the leanest grade of beef, followed by "choice" and "prime." Another rule of thumb: Any meat with the word "round" (eye of round, top round, ground round) or "loin" (tenderloin, sirloin) is generally a leaner cut. Other lean cuts are filet mignon and flank steak. Trim visible fat from meat, and skim congealed fat from the surface of cooled broths and meat juices.

- Eat chicken without the skin. (You can leave the skin on while cooking to help keep the meat moist, then remove it before eating.)

- Eat white-meat poultry instead of dark, which has more than twice as much saturated fat.

- Choose lower-fat versions of dairy foods. Fat-free milk, for example, has virtually no fat, while whole milk gets almost half of its fat calories from saturated fat. Skim milk is also an excellent choice, and all milk sold in Canada is fortified with the fat-soluble vitamin D.

FAVOR OILS, NUTS, AND FISH

Not all fat is bad for your heart or your insulin sensitivity (although it's all high in calories). In fact, some fat—the unsaturated kind—is actually good for you. This type of fat lowers your "bad" cholesterol rather than raising it. And there's more. A type of unsaturated fat called monounsaturated fat has even been shown to help reduce insulin resistance and make blood sugar easier to control. You can find it in:

- Almonds and other nuts
- Avocados
- Olive and canola oil
- Peanuts and peanut butter
- Seeds

Good news? Yes. But you'll still have to watch how much you eat, because at 9 calories per gram, even "good" fat can pack on the kilograms. By the way, peanut butter makes an excellent protein choice for quick lunches and snacks, but limit yourself to 2 tablespoons.

Fatty fish are another source of good fats. Called omega-3 fatty acids, they're the kind proven to cut the risk of a fatal heart attack—so people with diabetes should eat them! You'll find them in:

- Oily, cold-water fish such as salmon, tuna, canned sardines, and mackerel. Using the Plate Approach, you should aim to fill the protein quarter of your plate with fish two or three times a week.

- Shellfish such as shrimp, lobster, and mussels. They have smaller amounts of omega-3's but are low in saturated fat and calories. They also contain other nutrients that are important to people with diabetes, including vitamin B_{12} and zinc.

- Flaxseed and flax meal. Add them to cereal and homemade breads and other baked goods.

MAKE SURE DAIRY IS ON THE MENU

Dairy deserves special mention because foods such as low-fat cheese and fat-free milk and yogurt are high in both protein and calcium. Why is calcium important? Studies find that making sure you get adequate amounts can help you lose weight. The reason: A lack of adequate calcium triggers the release of a hormone called calcitriol, which prompts the body to store fat. Eating two or three servings of calcium-rich dairy foods per day helps keep calcitriol levels low so your body burns more fat and stores less. Taking calcium supplements doesn't seem to produce the same effect, which leads researchers to conclude that dairy foods may have some other, as-yet-undiscovered weight-loss advantage as well.

Not everyone tolerates the lactose in milk well, but if you're bothered by symptoms such as bloating and gas, you can ease dairy into your diet by having small amounts with meals, which slows the rate at which lactose enters your system. You can also forgo milk in favor of dairy foods that are naturally lower in lactose, such as low-fat cheese and yogurt.

Succeeding with Soul Food

Shirley Smith already loved vegetables when she joined the DO IT study—but that wasn't helping her lose weight or control her diabetes. "I liked collard greens, kale, and other traditional African-American dishes," she says, "just the way my mother made them—cooked with fatback, ham hocks, or salt pork." These fat-laden cooking techniques and a love of fried chicken (especially dark meat, the fattiest kind), dinner rolls, and desserts such as sweet potato pie boosted her weight to 99 kg (218 lb) and her blood sugar levels into the red zone of 11 mmol/L.

The Plate Approach helped Smith, an assistant professor of nursing, rethink her meals, starting with smaller portions in the carbohydrate and protein quarters. "I cut back on meat and rolls quite a bit," she says. "Eating chicken at home, I'd normally have the leg and thigh, but now I just have one piece. And if I'm served chicken breast at a conference, I'll only eat half of it, skip the roll, and eat all of the salad."

Eating fewer carbs and less protein automatically left more room for vegetables—but in her case, the vegetables themselves needed a fix. Her solution: replacing high-fat meats such as ham hocks with smoked turkey parts. "I simmer the turkey in water on low for, oh, probably 45 minutes, then I put the greens in and cook slowly for hours, the way my mother showed me," she says. "I add celery and onions to make it more tasty. It's very good." Just as important, she started eating more salads and fruit, which she always liked but wasn't accustomed to having. Now, she typically eats two servings of vegetables with lunch and dinner, so they make up about half the amount of food in her meals.

By taking steps like these (along with getting regular exercise and not skipping breakfast), Smith lost 16 percent of her body weight and dropped her blood sugar well into the normal range of 5. Understanding that no food is completely off-limits, she still sometimes cooks her greens the traditional way, "but I save that for special occasions like Thanksgiving and Christmas," she says, "and then I'll eat less pie." Although her weight and blood sugar have fluctuated with stress and age (she's 68), she's kept both below what they were when she started the plan three years ago. "The plan taught me a lot about how to eat, especially what an impact eating lots of fruits and vegetables can have," she says. "And I found that it works."

STEP 3 master your portions

The Plate Approach cuts calories simply and significantly by confining higher-calorie foods such as meat and starches to half of your plate. But how high should you heap those potatoes, and just how big is a proper portion of beef or chicken? What if you're not dining on a plate at all? Can the breakfast muffin you eat on a napkin or the sandwich you pack for lunch be as mighty as you like? Not exactly.

This chapter will help you get a handle on portions—and implement the Plate Approach—by showing you a generous sampling of real-life, easy-to-make meals.

These breakfasts, lunches, and dinners represent the perfect balance of vegetables (or fruit), carbohydrates, and protein, all in proper portion sizes. We even give you healthy, low-calorie snacks, desserts, and holiday menus tailor-made for people with diabetes. These meals prove that eating well doesn't mean enjoying your food any less.

You know by now that if you want to lose weight and bring your blood sugar down, you have to pay attention to what you eat. But what about *how much* you eat? It's not a point you can afford to ignore, although most people underestimate its importance. In one recent American survey, a whopping 78 percent of respondents said that eating certain types of food was more important for losing weight than eating fewer calories. It's little wonder that so many of us are still fighting the fat demon.

In case we haven't said it enough, we'll say it again: The key to losing weight is eating fewer calories (and burning more calories through exercise). The Plate Approach builds in calorie control by assigning carbs and protein—which provide most of our calories—to their quarter-plate positions. But it still helps to have a grasp of what a proper serving size is.

Figuring out how much food to buy and cook so that your plate is divided as it should be takes a little practice. Use the chart on page 85 to help you, and keep referring to it for as long as you need to. Eventually, serving and eating food in these portions will become second nature.

Perfect Portions
All Day, Every Day

BREAKFAST

Breakfast is the most important meal of your day. Aim to get about 350 calories to kick things off—and don't shy away from heartier foods such as waffles. Remember that having more calories in the morning can help you eat less later on.

One challenge with breakfast is getting protein into your meal. The breakfasts on the following pages all give you the protein you need, even when you're not sitting down to an omelet. Milk, yogurt, and peanut butter fit the bill. (For the fastest complete breakfast possible, grab a container of fat-free, sugar-free fruit yogurt and top it with 3 to 4 tablespoons of high-fiber cereal.)

A word about fruit juice: Stick to three quarters of a cup. Although it does contain important nutrients, juice is a concentrated source of calories, and it lacks the fiber that makes fresh fruit filling. All that natural sugar with little fiber to slow its digestion also means juice may send your blood sugar soaring.

Finally, if you decide to have plain old cereal instead of the breakfasts here, look for a brand that contains 5 or more grams of fiber per serving. Some brands also include a substantial amount of protein in the form of soy. Just top with fruit, and you'll have a perfect Plate Approach meal.

LUNCH

What makes a perfect lunch? Eating it absolutely no more than 5 hours after breakfast (and preferably sooner), for starters. You also want a meal that will energize you rather than send you into an afternoon slump. That means one with ample protein but little fat. The lunches on the following pages provide a healthy balance of nutrients and are easy to prepare.

You probably have a little more time for lunch than for breakfast, so don't rush: Slowly savoring your food will make you feel more satisfied, so you'll be less likely to overeat.

To make sure you get plenty of vegetables, add a salad or load up your sandwich with lettuce and tomato or cucumbers, bean sprouts, onions, or roasted red peppers from a jar. A piece of fruit is the simplest and smartest dessert.

DINNER

Most people think of dinner as the day's main meal, but the feasts we've come up with are designed (for the most part) to provide no more calories than the meals you eat for lunch. In fact, you can think of these as lunch previews, since all of them are perfect for reheating and eating as leftovers another day. Remember: Finish eating dinner at least 4 hours before bedtime to give your body time to digest your meal and use up most of those calories before your metabolism slows down for the night. Some of our fastest meals involve little more than throwing ingredients together. In general, if you need to get dinner on in a hurry, start with a bag of frozen stir-fry vegetables and go from there.

SNACKS

Healthy snacks can demand some advance planning; vending machines certainly don't offer a lot of options. In fact, it's not a bad idea to dump the whole concept of "snack foods," which typically includes chips, crackers, and candies. What does that

A Visual Guide to Portion Sizes

MEASUREMENT	PICTURE IT AS	USE FOR
1 cup	Clenched fist, 2 hands cupped	Milk and yogurt, beverages, cereal, rice (entrée), pasta (entrée), salad, pudding, mixed dishes (chili, stew, macaroni and cheese), Chinese food
½ cup	1 hand cupped	Pasta (side dish), rice (side dish), potatoes, fruit, hot cereal, beans, cottage cheese, coleslaw, potato salad
170 g (6 oz) (daily amount)	Cell phone, package of small recipe cards, chequebook	Fish, chicken, turkey, pork, beef, ham (if eaten once a day)
90 g (3 oz) (meal amount)	Palm of hand, deck of cards	Fish, chicken, turkey, pork, beef, ham (if eaten twice a day)
30 g (1 oz)	4 dice	Cheese, nuts
1 tablespoon	Thumb from knuckle to tip	Salad dressing, whipped topping, cream cheese, peanut butter, dip

leave? Plenty. Reach into your pantry or refrigerator for small helpings of foods that are staples of regular meals, such as vegetables, fruit, yogurt, and cereal. Then branch out to nuts or low-fat frozen treats. The snacks on the following pages make great hunger stoppers that are easy to carry with you or stash in a cooler (or small office fridge) and weigh in at 150 calories or less. Another option if you're near a microwave is a cup (that's 1 cup) of any soup that isn't cream based.

Remember, on the 10 Percent Plan, we *want* you to snack once or twice a day. Snacking is a great way to keep hunger and blood sugar under control and help you lose weight.

HOLIDAY MEALS

Holidays mean celebration, and there's nothing like a party to send your eating into overdrive. That's true whenever food becomes the focal point of socializing, but especially when eating is linked with time-honored tradition. Fortunately, you don't have to abandon any family rituals to keep calories under control. Watching portion sizes and passing up seconds will go a long way, but the real trick is to prepare foods in ways that keep fat to a minimum. Low-fat entrées such as turkey breast, lean ham, and chicken breast give you a big head start right out of the gate. From there, focus your attention on making smart choices with side dishes and desserts.

WEEKEND BREAKFAST

2-egg omelet filled with ½ cup vegetables (such as sautéed onions, green peppers, and mushrooms), topped with 30 g (1 oz) shredded fat-free sharp cheddar cheese

1 slice whole wheat toast with 1 teaspoon light tub margarine

¾ cup calcium-fortified orange juice

Calories: 350

breakfast

AT-YOUR-DESK DAY STARTER

1 whole wheat bagel 8-cm (3-in.) topped with 2 tablespoons peanut butter

1 medium banana

1 cup black or green tea

Calories: 405

BRIEFCASE BREAKFAST

1 hardboiled egg

1 low-fat Bran Muffin 5 cm (2 in.)
recipe on page 243

¾ cup cranberry juice

Calories: 310

Most of us have more leisure time on weekends, so take advantage of it by whipping up a tasty, vegetable-filled omelet. Eggs provide plenty of protein and as much as half your daily quota of vitamin B_{12}, which may protect against diabetes-related neuropathy. Egg yolks also have modest amounts of zinc, which helps protect cells in the pancreas that make insulin. No time to chop? Buy precut vegetables.

TIPS

▶ For a lower-calorie omelet, use 1 egg and 2 egg whites. It will look and taste the same.

▶ Add or substitute in-season vegetables such as zucchini, broccoli, or chopped spinach or tomatoes.

▶ Top with salsa and serve in a flour tortilla (forgo the toast) for a breakfast burrito.

You dash off to work without breakfast. No problem—if you have emergency rations such as peanut butter and small or mini-bagels or rice cakes stashed in your desk. Just grab the banana on your way out the door. Peanut butter is an excellent protein source that's easy to fit into your morning (but it's high in calories, so stick with 2 tablespoons), and tea is rich in antioxidants that help protect you from heart disease.

TIPS

▶ Beware of full-size bagels, which amount to four servings of carbohydrate and have twice the calories of 8-cm (3-in.) bagels.

▶ Bagels becoming boring? Substitute two rice cakes, which contain fewer calories and come in a variety of flavors, such as cinnamon and chocolate.

▶ Buy light peanut butter; it's an easy way to cut fat and calories. Just check the label to make sure it's actually lower in calories.

breakfast

Here's a meal you can grab and eat on the go. Just peel the egg before you leave the house and put it in a plastic sandwich bag. Watch out for store-bought muffins, which are gigantic calorie traps. Choose a small, low-fat muffin, or bake your own. Our recipe packs plenty of fiber and fruit with very little fat.

TIPS

▶ To enjoy eggs and protect your heart at the same time, buy eggs enhanced with omega-3 fatty acids—the same kind of fat found in salmon.

▶ As an alternative to fruit juice, substitute whole fruit, such as a handful of seedless purple grapes.

▶ To cut calories further, choose light cranberry juice or other juices that are lower in sugar and calories.

SPECIAL TREAT BREAKFAST

2 toasted low-fat frozen waffles topped with ½ cup fresh fruit and 1 tablespoon chopped pecans

½ cup fat-free milk

Calories: 355

WORKDAY BREAKFAST

1 fried egg between 2 English muffin halves, with sliced tomato and 30 g (1 oz) reduced-fat cheddar cheese

¾ cup orange juice

Calories: 340

QUICK AND EASY SUGAR BLASTER

1 package unsweetened instant oatmeal topped with ½ teaspoon cinnamon, 2 tablespoons craisins or raisins, and 1 tablespoon chopped walnuts

1 cup fat-free milk

Calories: 335

For times when you want something sweet, here's a meal that tastes like dessert. Surprised to see waffles? Don't be: Despite their reputation for being loaded with unhealthy fat, they easily fit into the plan if you choose low-fat varieties containing 3 g or less of fat per serving. Topping them with fruit instead of syrup dodges empty calories, and nuts add protein as well as heart-healthy monounsaturated fat.

TIPS

▸ Skip the milk and, for about the same number of calories, slather waffles and fruit with fat-free, sugar-free yogurt.

▸ Choose whole grain waffles for a fiber bonus.

▸ Vary the types of fruit and nuts you put on top to keep breakfast interesting. Blueberries, strawberries, raspberries, and other berries are loaded with antioxidants to fight off disease, so they offer a nutritional bonus.

This is just like a drive-through breakfast, but with fewer calories and a vegetable serving (the tomato). Choose whole wheat English muffins for extra fiber. If you haven't tasted reduced-fat cheese in a while, try it again; the products have improved greatly in terms of taste and texture.

TIPS

▸ Instead of frying the egg in butter or margarine, use a nonstick skillet with a little cooking spray.

▸ For an egg sandwich "Florentine" style, add steamed spinach.

breakfast

You know oatmeal is good for you: It's loaded with fiber and clears out cholesterol. But the biggest surprise benefit of this breakfast is that the cinnamon you add for flavor may naturally—and significantly—lower blood sugar in people with type 2 diabetes. And it's famous among cooks for giving the impression of sweetness without adding calories.

TIPS

▸ Add the milk before you cook the oatmeal rather than after: Instant oatmeal tends to be thin, and cooking it with milk will make it creamier.

▸ Use old-fashioned or quick-cooking oatmeal rather than instant for slightly more fiber and a heartier texture.

▸ Substitute slices of fresh banana or strawberries for the dried fruit.

SENSUOUS SALAD

2 to 3 cups salad greens topped with 90 g (3 oz) grilled chicken and ½ cup grilled vegetables (such as onions, portobello mushrooms, and green and red peppers)

1 small whole grain roll

Calories: 265

CHAMPIONSHIP CHILI

1 bowl (about 1½ cups)
  Hearty Turkey Chili
  recipe on page 239

2 or 3 whole wheat crackers

Calories: 185 plus crackers

BROWN-BAG SPECIAL

60 g (2 oz) peppered turkey breast and 1 slice part-skim mozzarella or reduced-fat cheddar cheese on 2 slices whole grain bread

Tossed salad with 1 tablespoon low-fat dressing

1 medium apple

Calories: 425

This salad has it all: Lean chicken breast for protein as well as plenty of antioxidant-rich vegetables. Grilling the vegetables—either on an outdoor grill or under the broiler—brings out rich flavor and natural sweetness. You can top the salad with 1 tablespoon of low-fat dressing if you like, although we think it has plenty of flavor on its own.

TIPS

▸ Instead of a roll, use a whole grain tortilla and roll up the salad ingredients for a tasty fajita.

▸ Other vegetables that are great grilled are eggplant, zucchini, and asparagus.

▸ No time to grill veggies? Crack open a jar of roasted peppers and a can of artichoke hearts.

High in fiber and low in fat, beans are the perfect food for people with diabetes. And if chili cook-offs gave awards for nutrition, you'd win top honors with this hearty dish made with ground turkey and plenty of vegetables. There's more than enough fiber and protein here to fill you up until dinner (with a small snack in between, of course!).

TIPS

▸ Substitute any type of beans you like for the kidney beans, such as black, pinto, or cannellini beans.

▸ Meatless soy crumbles provide all the protein of ground turkey and the mouthfeel of ground meat. Try them for a change of pace to cut cholesterol and saturated fat.

lunch

Add spice to a traditional brown-bag lunch by lining your whole grain bread with extra-flavorful peppered turkey. Add some reduced-fat cheese and a smear of mustard, and you have a meal with plenty of protein but almost no fat. The side salad and fruit (save it for dessert) fill out the produce section of your "plate."

TIPS

▸ For a hot version, grill the sandwich until the cheese melts.

▸ Replace the turkey with any other sandwich meat with 3 g of fat or less per serving.

▸ Eating on the go? Grab raw vegetables such as peppers, celery, and carrots instead of the salad.

▸ Use light bread to cut bread calories in half.

FORBIDDEN FAVORITE

1 pita pizza (topped with ½ cup broccoli, 60 g (2 oz) part-skim mozzarella, and 2 tablespoons tomato sauce)

Tossed salad with 1 tablespoon low-fat dressing

Calories: 315

recipe on page 225

lunch

A TASTE OF FRANCE

Tuna Salad Provençale
recipe on page 225

Calories: 340

REMADE REUBEN

Mock Reuben sandwich (60 g [2 oz] lean baked ham, 1 slice part-skim mozzarella, 2 tablespoons sauerkraut, 2 slices light rye bread, 2 teaspoons light tub margarine spread on the outside of the bread)

1 dill pickle

¾ cup Pineapple Coleslaw
recipe on page 233J94

Calories: 375

Who says you can't have pizza? True, pizza that's so greasy that the oil forms puddles is off-limits, but it's simple enough to make a good-for-you pizza at home. Loaded with vegetables, this is actually a perfect lunch when you're trying to control calories and blood sugar. If you opt for store-bought pizza, choose a thin-crust version, be sure to ask for vegetable toppings, and blot up excess oil with a paper towel.

TIPS

▶ Whip up a Mexican pizza by spreading a tortilla with fat-free refried beans, salsa, and reduced-fat cheese. Microwave for 90 seconds and top with shredded lettuce and chopped green onion and salsa or taco sauce if desired.

▶ If you're heating up a frozen pie that skimps on veggies, dress it up with sliced peppers and chopped spinach and olives.

Loaded with fiber, this salad, based on a dish from the south of France, shows how a simple can of tuna can become so much more with the help of an all-star medley of vegetables and a can of cannellini beans. Canned tuna is rich in vitamin B_{12}, which helps protect people with diabetes from nerve damage.

TIPS

▶ Buy tuna packed in water, not oil. It has far fewer calories and more heart-healthy omega-3 fats.

▶ For a special treat, use fresh grilled tuna.

lunch

The typical Reuben, piled high with corned beef, Swiss cheese, and Thousand Island dressing, is loaded with fat. This version offers the tangy taste with a fraction of the calories. You're better off without the Thousand Island dressing, but if you must have it, use a low-fat brand. Our Pineapple Coleslaw is made with a sugar substitute so you can indulge guilt-free. And unless you're watching your salt intake, feel free to feast on pickles—they have almost no calories.

TIPS

▶ When heating the sandwich on the stove, use medium heat, which will melt the cheese in about the same time it takes to lightly toast the bread.

▶ Coating the pan with cooking spray instead of using margarine on the bread will cut 60 calories.

▶ Choose bread with seeds to get more robust rye flavor and extra fiber.

FAST FALLBACK STIR-FRY

1 cup Shrimp and Vegetable Stir-Fry
recipe on page 222

½ cup brown rice

Calories: 266

dinner

MEAT-LOVER'S MEAL

140 g (5 oz) eye of round steak

¼ cup sautéed button mushrooms

1 medium baked potato topped with
2 tablespoons low-fat cottage
cheese or 1 tablespoon fat-free sour
cream

1 cup Zucchini and Tomato Casserole
recipe on page 230

Calories: 600

BACKYARD BARBECUE

110 g (4 oz) grilled chicken breast
with Cajun seasoning

1 cup steamed broccoli

Tossed salad with 3 sliced fresh
strawberries

1 medium ear of corn

Calories: 260

Once maligned, shrimp is actually a wonderful food that's rich in heart-healthy omega-3 fatty acids, packed with protein, and very low in fat. And making stir-fries is a great way to get dinner on the table fast, especially if you buy precut vegetables. Or you can keep a shrimp-and-vegetable frozen dinner on hand for harried nights and add extra frozen vegetables from a bag.

TIPS

▶ When choosing frozen dinners, look for brands that contain 300 calories or less and no more than 10 g of fat and 800 mg of sodium. Weight-loss brands usually fit the bill.

▶ For a bit more kick, add ½ teaspoon red pepper flakes and two chopped scallions.

▶ If you're watching your salt intake, always choose reduced-sodium soy sauce.

This dinner is higher in calories than other meals on our menu, but if you're a meat-and-potatoes kind of person, there's no reason you can't have them occasionally, as long as you consistently hold down calories at other times. The key is choosing a lean cut of meat, limiting your portion to about 140 g (5 oz), and keeping your baked potato topping light.

TIPS

▶ Low-fat cuts of meat include *loin* (tenderloin, sirloin), *round* (top round, eye of round, ground round, bottom round), *flank*, and *filet mignon*.

▶ Steer clear of *ribs* (spareribs, short ribs, ribeye, prime rib), *skirt steak*, and *brisket*.

▶ Trimmed ham, venison, veal, and lamb are generally lean.

dinner

Summertime, and the living is easy—and so is the cooking. Throw some chicken breasts on the barbie and sprinkle with Cajun seasoning for a fast and zesty meal. While you're at it, toss on some unhusked ears of corn. Put it all together with a tossed salad brightened with strawberries, and you've got a colorful, casual meal that's perfect for warm-weather entertaining.

TIPS

▶ If you must add some butter to your corn, use butter-flavored spray—no calories but lots of buttery flavor.

▶ Swap the corn for a small baked potato, which cooks on the grill (wrapped in foil) in about the same time as the chicken.

▶ Splash the salad with balsamic vinegar. It goes well with strawberries and adds no calories.

A TASTE OF ITALY

10-cm-square (4-in.-square) piece vegetable lasagna

Tossed salad with mandarin oranges and 1 tablespoon low-fat dressing

Calories: 300

OMEGA GLORY

170 g (6 oz) baked or grilled salmon

¾ cup sautéed greens

½ cup steamed carrots

½ cup Nutted Lemon Barley
  recipe on page 237

Calories: 395

dinner

QUICK-AND-EASY PRIMAVERA

Primavera (1 to 2 cups fresh or frozen stir-fry vegetables sautéed in garlic and oil, 90 g [3 oz] sliced chicken breast, ½ cup spaghetti, 1 teaspoon Parmesan cheese)

Tossed salad with 1 tablespoon low-fat dressing

Calories: 395

If you've been shunning lasagna because of its fat, put a meatless version on your A-list. Vegetables add color and bulk without the fat of meat. When time is tight, you can opt for frozen veggie lasagna instead of making it yourself. Just look for a low-fat brand. Toss mandarin oranges into your salad for a burst of color and sweetness.

TIPS

▸ Thawed frozen spinach and roasted peppers, zucchini, and eggplant make excellent fillings for vegetable lasagna.

▸ To satisfy meat lovers, add soy crumbles or veggie ground round. They mimic the texture and appearance of meat without the fat and cholesterol.

▸ Lasagna stands up well to freezing, so make extra. To freeze a whole pan of lasagna, bake it in a disposable aluminum baking pan and seal with foil.

The omega-3 fatty acids in fatty fish are so good for you, some doctors recommend that you have fish three times a week. Sautéed Swiss chard, kale, or collard greens provide a whopping dose of magnesium (low levels may be linked with diabetes), the antioxidant beta-carotene, and more than half your daily requirement of vitamin C. And barley is a rich source of cholesterol-lowering soluble fiber that deserves to be discovered.

TIPS

▸ For a change of pace, try mackerel, which is just as rich in omega-3's as salmon.

▸ Not a fan of leafy greens? Substitute green beans sprinkled with almonds.

dinner

You can make this meal using fresh vegetables, but there's certainly no shame in ripping open a bag of frozen stir-fry vegetables if you don't have much time. There's no sauce to make; just fry the vegetables quickly in a small amount of garlic and oil, toss in a bit of leftover grilled chicken, and sprinkle with Parmesan cheese.

TIPS

▸ Keep a jar of minced garlic on hand to add flavor to this dish and many others without adding fat.

▸ For a real flavor treat, buy a block of Parmesan cheese and grate or shred it yourself.

▸ Substitute chopped fresh asparagus or spinach for the mixed stir-fry vegetables.

SNOW-DAY STEW

1½ cups Beefy Mushroom-Barley Stew
recipe on page 240

Tossed salad with walnuts and raisins
and 1 tablespoon low-fat dressing

Calories: 360

PORK CHOPS TONIGHT

170 g (6 oz) center-cut pork loin
chops or pork tenderloin

¾ cup steamed green beans with
sliced almonds

1 small potato, sliced and roasted
with 1 teaspoon olive oil

Calories: 485

dinner

ONE-DISH DELIGHT

1½ cups Crab and Artichoke
Rice Skillet
recipe on page 223

5 steamed asparagus spears

Calories: 375

When the weather outside is frightful, nothing's more delightful than a hearty stew. It's an ideal way to get the robust flavor of meat without eating a lot of it—the chunky vegetables and thick, savory broth make it plenty satisfying, and red wine adds depth to the flavor. Barley thickens the stew while substantially boosting your fiber intake.

TIPS

▶ Jazz up leftovers by separating a roll of frozen low-fat biscuits and laying them on top of the stew in a casserole dish. Heat in the oven according to the biscuit directions and serve.

▶ If you like it, substitute stewing veal or venison, cut into 2-cm (1-in.) pieces, for the beef. Both are generally lower in fat than beef.

Pork loin or tenderloin is one of the leanest cuts of meat you can buy; if you trim off any visible fat, it's almost as lean as chicken breast. Pork contains zinc, which helps protect the insulin-making cells in the pancreas. A baked apple sprinkled with cinnamon—which may help control blood sugar—would be the perfect ending to this meal.

TIPS

▶ To ensure moist pork, choose thicker cuts, which retain their juices better.

▶ Sprinkle chops with thyme for extra flavor.

▶ If you like, substitute veal loin chops, which are also very lean.

▶ For more nutrients and a slower rise in blood sugar, trade the baked potato for a small sweet potato. Be sure to eat the skin, where fiber and nutrients are concentrated.

dinner

This sophisticated dish isn't cooked as much as assembled, which makes it super-fast and easy. All of the protein, vegetables, and carbohydrates you need are here in one dish. And the health benefits are considerable: Crab (even imitation crab) is low in fat and loaded with zinc, an important mineral for people with diabetes. Serve with brown rice instead of white to keep your blood sugar steadier.

TIPS

▶ Consider using fresh lump crabmeat, shrimp, or chicken instead of imitation seafood if you have high blood pressure; Imitation crab is higher in sodium than these other options.

▶ Add red and yellow peppers for an appealing splash of color and extra nutrients, such as vitamins C and A.

▶ Toss imitation crab with cocktail sauce and serve on a bed of lettuce for a quick, ready-to-eat salad.

CUBIST MASTERPIECE

Large bowl of sugar-free Jell-O cubes

Calories: 15

When you were a child, it jiggled and wiggled, and the entertainment factor alone was enough to make Jell-O special. Now that you're all grown up, Jell-O (the sugar-free kind) is still a great treat because you can eat it in almost unlimited amounts and not go overboard on calories.

desserts

I SCREAM, YOU SCREAM

Ice cream sundae (½ cup low-fat ice cream or frozen yogurt topped with 1 tablespoon fat-free caramel syrup)

Calories: 160

When the sun's beating down, you're sure to have ice cream on your mind. By choosing low-fat ice cream or frozen yogurt, you can cut the calories enough to indulge. Just put the container away once you've scooped out a proper serving.

PEACHY KEEN

1 cup Peach Crisp
recipe on page 246

Calories: 150

Sweet, spicy, smooth, and crunchy—this dessert's got it all (and good-for-you fruit to boot). Using a sugar substitute keeps the calories in check, and you can feel good about the oats and walnuts.

MELON MELODY

3 slices each of honeydew, cantaloupe, and mango

Calories: 95

As with a simple song, the biggest pleasure sometimes comes from the clarity and purity of just a few elements. With melons carrying the tune and mango providing a lively harmony, this dessert is pared to the basics yet still elegant and delightful.

GREEN WITH ENVY

1 cup Key Lime–Yogurt Mousse
recipe on page 244

Calories: 70

Are you ever tempted to reach across the table to try someone else's dessert? That's the feeling you'll get from this simple but deliciously tangy treat made with sugar-free key lime yogurt and fat-free whipped topping. Fortunately, you don't have to sneak a bite—it's all yours.

desserts

CHOCOLATE DELIGHT

1 cup Chocolate–Banana Pudding Parfait
recipe on page 244

Calories: 150

If you serve this to friends, you'd better reassure them: No, this doesn't mean you've given up on eating right. They'll nod and take a spoonful—and you'll have to reassure them again. Made with sugar-free chocolate pudding and fat-free whipped topping, this tastes infinitely more sinful than it is.

NUTS FOR PEANUTS

30 g (1 oz) peanuts

Calories: 165

The bargain lover in you will appreciate the dense, filling nutrition you can get from a relatively small serving of peanuts. Full of protein and "good" fats, the nuts actually appear to help people lose weight. Feel free to substitute a palmful of almonds or a tablespoon of peanut butter.

snacks

ALL STRUNG OUT

30 g (1 oz) fat-free string cheese

Calories: 80

Whoever invented string cheese was on to something: These portable snacks are satisfying and full of protein—and they contain no carbs!

CINEMATIC LICENSE

4 cups air-popped popcorn

Calories: 100

Who says popcorn is only for the movies? Take popcorn out of the multiplex and have it as a light snack. Why not? It's low in calories and high in fiber.

A CALL TO GRAPENESS

20 red seedless grapes

Calories: 100

Grapes are full of water, which makes them automatically low in calories. Twenty grapes registers in your brain as lots of separate items, and popping them into your mouth one by one makes you feel that you're getting more food than you really are.

VEGGIE VARIETY PACK

1 to 2 cups sliced raw vegetables

Calories: 35

Think of vegetables as sociable foods: They hate to be alone. Even when you snack, you'll have a livelier time if you throw veggies together and let their tastes mingle. Soft and crunchy, watery and dense, this combination makes for a pleasing mix.

snacks

OH, FUDGE

1 frozen fudge bar

Calories: 80

No regrets here: Although it seems like an indulgence (go ahead—let yourself think of it as one), a frozen fudge bar contains remarkably few calories for the amount of chocolate enjoyment you get. To cut calories in half, choose a sugar-free brand.

THANKSGIVING DINNER

170 g (6 oz) turkey breast

½ cup Sage Dressing (stuffing)
recipe on page 236

2 tablespoons fat-free gravy

½ cup Praline Sweet Potato Casserole
recipe on page 236

2 tablespoons cranberry relish

½ cup Green Bean Casserole
recipe on page 230

Calories: 630

holiday meals

CHRISTMAS DINNER

170 g (6 oz) lean baked ham

½ cup Scalloped Potatoes
recipe on page 234

½ cup Green Peas and Onions
recipe on page 231

½ cup Waldorf Salad
recipe on page 224

Calories: 550

CANADA DAY PICNIC

225 g (8 oz) Hickory-Smoked
Barbecued Chicken
recipe on page 219

½ cup German Potato Salad
with Dijon Vinaigrette
recipe on page 234

½ cup baked beans

½ cup Ambrosia Fruit Salad
recipe on page 246

7-cm-thick (3-in.-thick) slice watermelon

Calories: 530

The symbol of Thanksgiving may be the horn of plenty, but there's no reason you need to eat plenty of fat. Turkey is going to be the star of your plate, and that's just fine because it's low in fat if you stick to white meat and keep the portion size to a reasonable 170 g (6 oz) .And the traditional Thanksgiving side dishes? These versions were designed to be lower in fat and calories.

TIPS

▶ Afraid you'll overeat? Munch a healthy snack, such as celery sticks, before dinner. (You probably have celery left over from making the stuffing.)

▶ Avoid pecan pie; it's a virtual calorie bomb. Choose our reduced-calorie Pumpkin Pie on page 247 or our Apple Pie on page 125 instead.

The savory smell of lean baked ham filling the air is just part of what makes this meat a perfect centerpiece for all your Christmas homecomings. Both lean and succulent, ham has an abundance of flavor but can be sliced thin to keep taste satisfaction high and calories low. Side dishes are dominated by vegetables that you can keep replenishing as you linger around the table with laughter and conversation.

TIPS

▶ Save the hot toddies and wine for after dinner. That way, the alcohol won't weaken your resolve not to overeat, plus you'll drink fewer empty calories if you already feel full.

▶ Can't keep your hands out of the mixed nuts? Fill the bowl with nuts in their shells and use a traditional nutcracker. The effort will slow you down and make you more mindful of how much you're eating.

holiday meals

Get out the grill for our national birthday celebration and wow your friends and family with this hickory-smoked barbecued chicken. It takes a bit more preparation than typical slap-it-on-the-barbie fare, but the aroma of the sauce will make your patio a magnet even for the neighbors you didn't invite. Make up for your effort by simply opening a can of baked beans. Serve with two perfect summer salads.

TIPS

▶ Choose the breast and remove the skin to cut calories significantly.

▶ To cut grilling time—and possibly cancer-causing chemicals that can arise from grilling—partially precook the chicken in the microwave. For cut-up parts, microwave on high for 3 to 4 minutes, then finish on the grill.

STEP 4 master your disaster foods

A key aspect of the 10 Percent Plan is that you never have to do without foods you love. (Otherwise, frankly, the chances that you'd stick with the plan would be slim.) If you're like most people, though, a lot of the dishes on your list of favorites are dietary disasters loaded with fat and calories. An insurmountable problem? Hardly.

On the following pages, you'll find recipes for more than a dozen classic favorites, from burgers and fries to pizza and cheesecake, that have been modified to substantially cut fat and calories while preserving the flavors you love.

It's time to stop thinking of good-tasting food as a stumbling block. If you love macaroni and cheese or chicken wings, you don't have to deprive yourself. These lower-calorie versions let you indulge—in moderation, of course—without the guilt.

How can you take a meal such as a hamburger and French fries and make it better for you? The most obvious answer is to cut some of the fat, the double-barreled nutrient that has more than twice the calories of carbs or protein. (It will also help to keep portions small and round out your meal with plenty of vegetables.)

Truth be told, fat gets more credit for taste than it deserves. In many cases, it's texture you want (creamy, meaty, crunchy), not the fat itself. In other cases, fat is mere baggage—an ingredient that happens to come with some foods, such as dairy products and certain cuts of meat, but not others.

We pared these worst-offender recipes of much of their fat and threw in a few other key calorie-saving changes to boot. The best part is, you still get great taste. Can you give the same treatment to other favorite foods? Absolutely. Just use the following culinary "special effects."

- Substitute leaner meats for fattier ones, such as white-meat poultry for dark, lean ground turkey for ground beef, or pork tenderloins for ribs.

- Bake or broil instead of frying in oil, which saturates whatever you're cooking, especially if the food is breaded.

- Remove skin from poultry, trim visible fat from meat, and throw out the egg yolks. Why worry about hidden fat when the fat you can see—and remove—does most of the harm?

- Buy low-fat or sugar-free products. If you haven't recently tried low-fat or fat-free foods (especially cheese), try them again: They've gotten better. If one brand doesn't taste good to you, try another. And you'll always save calories by replacing whole milk with fat-free or using naturally lower-fat cheeses such as mozzarella instead of higher-fat ones such as cheddar.

- Mix higher-fat meats, cheeses, and other foods with lower-fat versions if you don't want to make wholesale substitutions.

Cutting a few calories at every meal will add up to real calorie savings. Once you have cut 3,500 calories, you'll have lost 450 g (1 lb) of fat. Now, to find specific solutions for some of your favorite foods, check out the recipes starting on the next page.

▶**TIP** If you prefer the taste of white-bread buns, check your supermarket bread aisle for "lite," "diet," or "low-carb" buns, which are slightly smaller, have fewer calories, and contain more fiber than regular buns.

▶**TIP** To get crispy fries without adding significant calories or fat, toss them in egg whites before baking. The whites form a crust that gets crunchy when heated.

Hamburgers

No North American menu is complete without the classic burger. But a third of a typical hamburger's calories come from saturated fat, so make this meal dramatically healthier by choosing leaner beef, going halvesies with ground turkey, and bulking up the meat with mushrooms and high-fiber oats.

250 g (½ lb) ground round

250 g (½ lb) ground turkey

½ cup finely chopped mushrooms

¼ cup oats or bread crumbs

2 tablespoons finely chopped onion

6 whole grain buns

Lettuce (optional)

Tomato slices (optional)

1. Combine the beef, turkey, mushrooms, oats or bread crumbs, and onion in a large bowl. Form into 6 patties.

2. Grill or broil the patties until cooked through. Serve on the buns with the lettuce and tomato, if desired.

DISASTER FOOD	MASTER FOOD
500 g (1 lb) regular ground beef	500 g (1 lb) low-fat ground round and ground turkey with oats and chopped mushrooms
Regular bun	Whole grain bun
Calories per serving: 465	Calories per serving: 225
Fat per serving: 22 g	Fat per serving: 8 g

French Fries

What burger is complete without fries? The trouble is, soft-fleshed potatoes are grease sponges, and deep-frying more than triples calories. Solution: Make fries satisfyingly crispy by baking with high heat.

1 medium potato (about 170 g/6 oz)

Seasoned salt (optional)

1. Pierce the potato and microwave for about 4 minutes. Set aside until cool enough to handle.

2. Preheat the oven to 260°C (500°F). Spray a baking sheet with cooking spray.

3. Cut the potato into strips and arrange in a single layer on the baking sheet. Lightly spray the tops with cooking spray and sprinkle with the seasoned salt, if desired.

4. Bake, turning once, until brown and crisp, about 10 minutes.

DISASTER FOOD	MASTER FOOD
Fried potatoes	Baked potatoes
Cooked in oil	Coated with cooking spray
Calories per serving: 400	Calories per serving: 90
Fat per serving: 20 g	Fat per serving: 0 g

master your disaster foods

▲ Macaroni and Cheese

SERVES 6

Bet you never thought a creamy dish could be low in fat—but this version is. Calorie savings, though significant, aren't enormous, but you dramatically cut saturated fat— the dangerous kind that makes blood sugar control more difficult and increases the risk of heart disease.

3 tablespoons light tub margarine

¼ cup all-purpose flour

¾ teaspoon mustard powder

2 cans (385 ml each) fat-free evaporated milk

¼ cup Parmesan cheese

1 cup shredded fat-free sharp cheddar cheese

½ teaspoon salt

¼ teaspoon fresh-ground black pepper

5 cups cooked elbow macaroni

Pinch paprika

1. Preheat the oven to 180˚C (350˚F). Lightly grease a 3-L (13 x 9 x 3-in.) baking dish.

2. Melt the margarine in a large, heavy saucepan over low heat. Add the flour and stir until blended.

3. Add the mustard. Gradually add the evaporated milk, stirring constantly with a wire whisk, and cook for 2 minutes. Cook over medium heat, stirring constantly, until slightly thickened and bubbling, about 10 minutes. Remove from the heat.

4. Add the Parmesan, cheddar, salt, and pepper and stir until the cheese melts.

5. Stir in the macaroni and pour into the baking dish. Sprinkle lightly with the paprika. Bake until bubbling, about 30 minutes.

DISASTER FOOD	MASTER FOOD.
3 tablespoons butter	3 tablespoons light margarine
2 cups whole milk	2 cans fat-free evaporated milk
2 cups full-fat shredded cheese	1 cup fat-free shredded cheese and ¼ cup Parmesan cheese
Calories per serving: 388	Calories per serving: 325
Fat per serving: 21 g	Fat per serving: 3.5 g

master your disaster foods

Eggplant Parmesan

SERVES 8

When eggplant is breaded and deep-fried, its sponginess makes it soak up fat and oil. This baked version, however, is wonderfully cheesy and saucily seasoned, with two-thirds fewer calories than usual.

2 medium eggplants, peeled and sliced 1 cm (½ in.) thick

2 teaspoons garlic powder

Salt, to taste (optional)

Fresh-ground black pepper, to taste (optional)

2 cups marinara or tomato sauce

1 cup shredded part-skim mozzarella cheese

½ cup Italian-style dried bread crumbs

¼ cup grated Parmesan cheese

1 tablespoon minced parsley

1. Preheat the broiler. Spray a 3-L (13 x 9 x 3-in.) baking dish with cooking spray.

2. Sprinkle the eggplant with the garlic powder, then the salt and pepper, if desired. Arrange the slices in a single layer on a baking sheet and spray with olive oil-flavored cooking spray. Broil 10 cm (4 in.) from the heat until soft, 5 minutes per side.

3. Change the oven temperature to 190°C (375°F). Layer one-third of the eggplant, sauce, and mozzarella in the baking dish, then repeat the layers two more times. Sprinkle the top with the bread crumbs and Parmesan. Bake until bubbling, about 30 minutes. Sprinkle with the parsley before serving.

DISASTER FOOD	MASTER FOOD
Deep-fried	Broiled and baked
¼ cup vegetable oil	Olive oil-flavored cooking spray
1 whole egg	No egg
170 g (6 oz) mozzarella cheese	110 g (4 oz) mozzarella cheese plus 30 g (1 oz) Parmesan cheese
Calories per serving: 300	Calories per serving: 200
Fat per serving: 18 g	Fat per serving: 6 g

▶TIP Cut calories—and simplify the recipe—by preparing just a single layer, which reduces the amount of cheese.

Oven "Fried" Chicken

SERVES 6

Most of the problems with standard fried chicken are only skin-deep. Pull off the skin and lighten the breading for a makeover that still gives you the savory, crispy taste you love.

6 boneless skinless chicken breast halves (about 700 g/1½ lb)

Salt, to taste (optional)

Fresh-ground black pepper, to taste (optional)

¼ cup fat-free milk

1 egg white, lightly beaten

½ cup cornflake crumbs

1. Preheat the oven to 200°C (400°F). Spray a baking sheet with cooking spray.

2. Rinse the chicken, pat dry, and season with the salt and pepper, if desired.

3. Combine the milk and egg white in a medium bowl. Place the cornflake crumbs in a shallow bowl or on a plate. Dip each chicken piece in the egg and milk, then roll in the cornflake crumbs until well coated.

4. Arrange the chicken pieces in a single layer on the baking sheet. Spray the tops with cooking spray and bake until brown and crisp, 20 to 30 minutes.

DISASTER FOOD	MASTER FOOD
Chicken parts with skin, including dark meat	Chicken breasts without skin
Breaded with beaten whole egg and bread crumbs	Coated with egg white and cornflake crumbs
Fried in shortening or oil	Coated with cooking spray and baked
Calories per serving: 545	Calories per serving: 175
Fat per serving: 38 g	Fat per serving: 3 g

Mashed Potatoes

SERVES 6

You can pare down the fat in this favorite side dish with just two smart substitutions. But don't undo your gains by smothering the potatoes with butter and gravy! Choose a modest amount of fat-free sour cream instead.

0.9 kg (2 lb) potatoes

¾ cup skim or fat-free milk, warmed

¼ cup butter-flavored sprinkles

Salt, to taste (optional)

Fresh-ground black pepper, to taste (optional)

1. Peel the potatoes, place in a saucepan, and add enough water to cover. Bring to a boil and cook until the potatoes are soft and the liquid is reduced to about 2 tablespoons, about 15 to 20 minutes. Remove from the heat.

2. Mash with an electric mixer.

3. Combine ½ cup of the milk and the butter-flavored sprinkles in a small bowl. Stir into the potatoes, adding more milk if necessary to reach the desired consistency. Season with the salt and pepper, if desired.

DISASTER FOOD	MASTER FOOD
3 tablespoons butter	¼ cup butter-flavored sprinkles
Whole milk	Skim or fat-free milk
Calories per serving: 220	Calories per serving: 145
Fat per serving: 8 g	Fat per serving: 1 g

▶**TIP** Substitute fat-free chicken broth for the milk in the mashed potatoes to save 50 more calories.

▶**TIP** Cut leftover chicken into strips, heat, and add to a large tossed salad or use in a sandwich on a whole grain bun with lettuce and tomato.

▶**TIP** When making your own dough, substitute whole wheat flour for about a third of the white flour to get an extra dose of fiber.

▲ Sausage and Vegetable Pizza

SERVES 4

A thin crust and low-fat cheese make this pizza a less guilty pleasure. Crumbled vegetarian breakfast "sausage" patties give you all the taste of sausage but almost none of the fat.

1 package pizza crust mix

1 cup low-fat pizza sauce

4 vegetarian sausage patties

1¼ cups thinly sliced bell pepper

½ cup sliced mushrooms

2 tablespoons chopped onion

½ cup thawed frozen chopped spinach

¾ cup shredded part-skim mozzarella cheese

1. Preheat the oven to 230°C (450°F). Spray a baking sheet with cooking spray.

2. Prepare the crust according to the package directions. Press the dough into a thin 30 x 35 cm (12 x 14-in.) rectangle on the baking sheet. Spread the sauce evenly on the crust and crumble the sausage over the sauce. Top with the pepper, mushrooms, onion, and spinach. Sprinkle with the cheese.

3. Bake on the lowest oven rack until the crust is brown, 12 to 17 minutes.

DISASTER FOOD	MASTER FOOD
2 cups provolone and 2 cups mozzarella cheese	¾ cup mozzarella cheese
Sausage	Vegetarian patties
Pepperoni	Peppers, mushrooms, onions, spinach
Calories per serving*: 795	Calories per serving*: 370
Fat per serving*: 42 g	Fat per serving*: 8 g
*two slices	

Buffalo Chicken Hot "Wings"

The secret of the zesty chicken wings famously created in a Buffalo, New York, pub 40 years ago was never the chicken but the sauce. Substitute chicken breast tenders for high-fat wings, and you'll keep the spicy flavor but lose most of the fat.

- **1 tablespoon light tub margarine**
- **0.5 kg (1 lb) chicken breast tenders or strips**
- **2 tablespoons hot red pepper sauce**
- **1½ teaspoons apple cider vinegar**
- **Salt, to taste (optional)**
- **Fresh-ground black pepper, to taste (optional)**

1. Melt the margarine in a medium nonstick skillet.

2. Add the chicken and brown over medium heat for about 5 minutes. Turn to brown the other side, about 3 minutes. Sprinkle the red pepper sauce and vinegar over the chicken and continue cooking until browned on all sides, about 5 minutes longer. Increase the heat to high and cook until the chicken is coated and the sauce is completely reduced, about 2 minutes. Season with the salt and pepper, if desired.

DISASTER FOOD	MASTER FOOD
Chicken wings	Boneless, skinless chicken breast strips
2 tablespoons butter	1 tablespoon light margarine
Deep-fried and flavored with sauce	Sautéed in red pepper sauce and light margarine
Calories per serving: 380 for 110 g (4 oz) (about 12 large wings)	Calories per serving: 140 for 110 g (4 oz) (about 4 tenders)
Fat per serving: 24 g	Fat per serving: 3 g

▶**TIP** Honor Buffalo tradition by serving blue cheese dressing for dipping—but choose a fat-free or low-fat version.

▶**TIP** Add extra mushrooms or chickpeas or broccoli to give the sauce more volume, which will make the dish more satisfying in smaller portions.

▶**TIP** Use fusilli, rigatoni, orecchiette, or other bulky pasta instead of spaghetti: Their airy shapes make your plate look fuller, so you eat fewer calories.

Spaghetti with "Meat" Sauce

SERVES 4

Half the joy of a good meat sauce is its crumbly, beefy texture. Get the effect of a meaty mouthful by using less ground round and adding veggie ground round or soy crumble. No one will notice the difference! Veggie ground round or soy crumble looks and tastes like cooked ground beef and is found in most supermarkets. Not sold on soy? Substitute 110 g (4 oz) of lean ground turkey breast.

225 g (8 oz) spaghetti

110 g (4 oz) ground round

1¼ cup diced onion

¼ cup chopped green bell pepper

⅔ cup (110 g/4 oz) veggie ground round or soy crumble

1 teaspoon minced garlic

110 g (4 oz) fresh mushrooms, sliced

1 can (213 ml) tomato sauce

1 can (796 ml) petite diced Italian-style tomatoes

1 tablespoon chopped parsley

½ teaspoon thyme, basil, and oregano

1. Cook the spaghetti according to the package directions. Drain and keep warm.

2. Meanwhile, brown the beef, onion, and pepper in a medium nonstick skillet until the meat is cooked through and the vegetables are tender, about 5 minutes.

3. Add the veggie ground round or soy crumble, garlic, and mushrooms and cook until heated through, about 3 minutes.

4. Add the tomato sauce, tomatoes, parsley, and spices and cook, stirring occasionally, for about 15 minutes. Serve over the spaghetti.

DISASTER FOOD	MASTER FOOD
Regular ground beef	Half soy crumbles and half ground round
250 g (½ lb) pork sausage	No sausage
Calories per serving: 625	Calories per serving: 350
Fat per serving: 30 g	Fat per serving: 6 g

"Fried" Fish Sandwich

High-protein fish is an excellent addition to your plate—but not when it's laden with oily breading and heavy helpings of tartar sauce. This finer fish dish solves those problems, providing only a fraction of the usual calories and fat without sacrificing crunch.

¼ cup skim or fat-free milk

½ cup cornflake crumbs

2 teaspoons paprika

1 tablespoon Old Bay seafood seasoning

500 g (1 lb) fish fillets

4 light hamburger buns

1. Preheat the oven to 230°C (450°F). Spray a baking sheet with cooking spray.

2. Place the milk in a small bowl. Combine the cornflake crumbs, paprika, and seafood seasoning in a small bowl, then spread on a plate. Dip each fillet in the milk and coat with the seasoned crumbs. Place the fillets in single layer on the baking sheet.

3. Bake until the fish flakes easily, about 10 minutes per inch of thickness.

DISASTER FOOD	MASTER FOOD
Breaded with egg batter	Coated with skim or fat-free milk and cornflake crumbs
Deep-fried	Baked
Flavored with tartar sauce	Flavored with seasoning and paprika
Regular bun	Light bun
Calories per serving: 720	Calories per serving: 275
Fat per serving: 40 g	Fat per serving: 3 g

▶TIP Can't do without tartar sauce? Whip up a low-fat version using 4 parts fat-free or light mayonnaise and 1 part pickle relish.

▶**TIP** Change the flavor by substituting canned chicken and low-fat cream of chicken soup for the tuna and cream of mushroom soup.

▲ Tuna-Noodle Casserole

SERVES 4

This family favorite tends to be loaded with fat, but that can easily be avoided with a few simple changes that won't significantly affect the creamy, savory flavor.

225 g (8 oz) broad egg noodles

110 g (4 oz) sliced, fresh mushrooms

1 can (320 ml) low-fat cream of mushroom soup

1 can (170 g) water-packed tuna, drained

½ cup fat-free milk

1 cup shredded fat-free cheddar cheese

1 cup frozen peas

1. Preheat the oven to 180°C (350°F).

2. Cook the noodles according to the package directions until firm-tender, then drain.

3. Combine the noodles, mushrooms, soup, tuna, milk, cheese, and peas in a 1.5-L (11 x 7-in.) baking dish. Bake until bubbling, about 30 minutes.

DISASTER FOOD	MASTER FOOD
1 can regular cream of mushroom soup	1 can low-fat cream of mushroom soup
2 cans oil-packed tuna	1 can water-packed tuna
2 eggs	No eggs
Whole milk	Fat-free milk
1½ cups shredded American cheese	1 cup shredded fat-free cheddar cheese
No vegetables	1 cup frozen peas
Calories per serving: 455	Calories per serving: 305
Fat per serving: 21 g	Fat per serving: 5.5 g

▶**TIP** Cut calories further by using fat-free milk or evaporated fat-free milk in place of 2%.

Vegetable Fettuccine Alfredo

SERVES 4

Fat-free half-and-half makes an ideal stand-in for the heavy cream typically used in this dish, while a medley of vegetables adds an appealing dash of color—and bulks up the dish so you can eat more for fewer calories.

340 g (12 oz) fettuccine

2 cups broccoli florets

225 g (8 oz) baby carrots, cut in half lengthwise

1 cup fresh or thawed frozen green peas

1 large red bell pepper, seeded and cut into thin strips

1 tablespoon light tub margarine

1 small clove garlic, minced

2 tablespoons all-purpose flour

½ teaspoon salt

1½ cups 2% milk

½ cup fat-free half-and-half

½ cup freshly grated Parmesan cheese

1. Cook the fettuccine according to the package directions. Drain and keep warm.

2. Meanwhile, bring a large saucepan of water to a boil and cook the broccoli and carrots for 5 minutes. Add the peas and pepper and cook 3 minutes longer. Drain and keep warm.

3. Melt the margarine in a medium saucepan over medium heat. Add the garlic and sauté until golden, about 2 minutes. Whisk in the flour and salt and cook until bubbling, about 2 minutes. Gradually whisk in the milk and half-and-half and bring to a boil. Reduce the heat and simmer, whisking constantly, until thick, 1 to 2 minutes.

4. Reduce the heat to low. Stir in the cheese until melted and smooth. Toss the fettuccine, vegetables, and sauce in large serving bowl.

DISASTER FOOD	MASTER FOOD
No vegetables	Carrots, broccoli, peas, red pepper, garlic
Heavy cream	Fat-free half-and-half
Egg yolks	No egg
1 cup Parmesan cheese	½ cup Parmesan cheese
2 tablespoons butter	1 tablespoon light margarine
Calories per serving: 1,140	Calories per serving: 540
Fat per serving: 87 g	Fat per serving: 10 g

Burgundy Beef Stew

SERVES 4

Using eye of round or top round makes this meal much lower in fat than traditional stew made with chuck. And because it's slow-cooked, the meat will be tender. Red wine lends a flavor right out of a French bistro and adds heart-protective antioxidants. A wealth of vegetables accented (not outnumbered) by beef cubes keeps calories under control.

340 g (12 oz) beef round, trimmed of all visible fat and cut into 1-cm (½-in.) chunks

1½ cups thawed frozen pearl onions

3 carrots, thinly sliced

4 cloves garlic, slivered

1 tablespoon sugar

450 g (16 oz) mushrooms, quartered

2 tablespoons all-purpose flour

½ cup dry red wine or chicken broth

¾ cup water

¾ teaspoon thyme

¾ teaspoon salt

½ teaspoon fresh-ground black pepper

1. Preheat the oven to 180°C (350°F).

2. Spray a nonstick Dutch oven or flameproof casserole with cooking spray. Add the beef and cook until brown, about 5 minutes. Transfer to a plate with a slotted spoon.

3. Add the onions, carrots, and garlic to the pan. Sprinkle with the sugar and cook until the onions are golden, about 7 minutes. Add the mushrooms and cook until tender, about 4 minutes.

4. Return the beef (and any accumulated juices) to the pan. Sprinkle with the flour and cook, stirring, until the flour is absorbed, about 3 minutes.

5. Add the wine or broth and bring to a boil. Add the water and seasonings and return to a boil. Cover and bake until the meat is tender, about 1 hour. (The stew can be made ahead and refrigerated. Reheat at 160°C [325°F].)

DISASTER FOOD	MASTER FOOD
Beef chuck browned with oil	Beef round browned with cooking spray
170 g (6 oz) beef per serving	85 g (3 oz) beef per serving
Potatoes	No potatoes and more vegetables
Calories per serving: 405	Calories per serving: 275
Fat per serving: 19 g	Fat per serving: 3.5 g

▶**TIP** Make the stew seem even beefier by adding meaty vegetables such as eggplant or sun-dried tomatoes.

▼ Enchiladas

Typically made with beef, this zesty Mexican-style recipe cuts fat by substituting turkey and uses lots of black beans to enhance the south-of-the-border flavor (along with the vegetable and fiber content).

2½ cups salsa

¼ cup chopped cilantro

1 teaspoon ground cumin

8 15-cm (6-in.) tortillas

225 g (8 oz) cooked turkey breast, shredded

¾ cup canned black beans, rinsed and drained

1 small red onion, finely chopped

1 cup shredded reduced-fat cheddar cheese

1. Preheat the oven to 180°C (350°F). Lightly spray a 1.5-L (7 x 11-in.) baking dish with cooking spray.

2. Combine the salsa, cilantro, and cumin in a shallow bowl at least 15 cm (6 in.) in diameter.

3. Dip a tortilla in the salsa mixture, coating completely. Place on a plate or sheet of wax paper. Top with 2 tablespoons of the salsa mixture, then with one-eighth of the turkey, beans, and onion. Sprinkle with 1 tablespoon of the cheese. Roll up and place seam-side down in the baking dish. Repeat with the remaining tortillas.

4. Spoon the remaining salsa mixture over the enchiladas and sprinkle with the remaining ½ cup cheese. Bake until bubbling, about 15 minutes.

DISASTER FOOD	MASTER FOOD
Skirt steak	Shredded turkey breast
1¼ cups regular cheddar cheese	1 cup reduced-fat cheddar cheese
No beans	Black beans
Calories per serving: 588	Calories per serving: 369
Fat per serving: 35 g	Fat per serving: 7 g

▶**TIP** Choose corn tortillas instead of flour tortillas, which contain more fat and calories. Or use fat-free flour tortillas.

► **TIP** Simplify the recipe by using center-cut pork and skipping the skewers. Coat the pork with sauce and bake until done, about 1 hour.

▲ Barbecued "Ribs"

SERVES 6

Meat doesn't get much fattier than pork ribs, but you can get the same barbecue flavor by substituting much leaner pork tenderloins. You'll cut fat calories by 90 percent.

2 **pork tenderloins (about 340 g/12 oz each), trimmed of all visible fat**

1 **medium red onion, chopped**

1 **medium red bell pepper, seeded and chopped**

3 **cloves garlic, minced**

1 **cup ketchup**

½ **cup chili sauce**

¼ **cup unsulfured molasses**

3 **tablespoons Worcester-shire sauce**

2 **tablespoons light brown sugar**

2 **teaspoons chili powder**

2 **teaspoons mustard powder**

Hot red pepper sauce, to taste

1. Soak four 30-cm (12-in.) wooden skewers in water for 30 minutes. Butterfly the pork, then cut into "ribs" and thread onto the skewers. Cover and refrigerate.

2. Place the oven rack in the upper third of the oven and preheat to 230°C (450°F). Lightly spray a jelly-roll pan with cooking spray. Spread the vegetables in the pan and lightly spray with cooking spray. Roast, tossing frequently, until brown and tender, about 15 minutes.

3. Transfer to a food processor. Add the ketchup, chili sauce, molasses, Worcestershire, sugar, chili powder, mustard, and red pepper sauce. Puree. Pour into a sauce-pan. Cover and cook over medium-low heat, stirring occa-sionally, until bubbling, about 15 minutes. Remove 1 cup sauce for basting and keep the remaining sauce hot.

4. Spray a grill rack or broiler pan generously with cooking spray and preheat the grill or broiler. Baste both sides of the pork with sauce. Grill or broil until cooked through, about 15 minutes, turning and basting every 4 minutes. Serve with the remaining sauce on the side.

DISASTER FOOD	MASTER FOOD
Pork ribs	Pork tenderloin
½ cup margarine	No margarine
½ cup brown sugar	2 tablespoons light brown sugar
Calories per serving: 665	Calories per serving: 284
Fat per serving: 45 g	Fat per serving: 4.5 g

▶TIP Some artificial sweeteners break down under high heat, so use brands such as Equal Spoonful or Splenda Granular for baking. (Equal Spoonful does break down under high heat except in fruit pies.) They measure the same as sugar.

◀ Apple Pie

This popular Canadian dessert doesn't have to be quintessentially fattening. This version has all the tart sweetness of the real-deal but only a third of the calories. Light margarine contains more water than regular margarine, so work quickly when rolling the dough so the margarine doesn't soften and make the dough sticky.

- 3 tablespoons light tub margarine
- ½ cup flour
- ¼ teaspoon salt
- 1 tablespoon canola oil
- 1½ tablespoons cold water
- 1 tablespoon quick-cooking tapioca powder
- 6 medium baking apples (such as Granny Smith or Macintosh), peeled, cored, and sliced (4–5 cups)
- ⅔ cup artificial sweetener
- ½–1 tablespoon ground cinnamon
- 1 teaspoon skim or fat-free milk (optional)

1. Preheat the oven to 180°C (350°F). Place the margarine in the freezer until very cold but not frozen.

2. Combine the flour and salt in a medium bowl. Cut in the chilled margarine with a pastry blender until the mixture resembles coarse meal. Add the oil and blend quickly. Sprinkle the water evenly over the flour and stir lightly with a fork until moistened.

3. Shape the dough into a ball and roll between 2 sheets of lightly floured wax paper, making a 25-cm (10-in.) circle about 3 mm (⅛ in.) thick.

4. Sprinkle the tapioca on the bottom of a 23 x 4-cm (9-in.) pie plate to absorb liquid from the apples during cooking. Add the apples and sweetener and sprinkle with the cinnamon. Place the crust over the apples. Crimp the edges to seal and cut slits in the top. Brush lightly with the milk, if desired. Bake until the crust is golden and a table knife inserted into center of the pie comes out easily, about 1 hour.

DISASTER FOOD	MASTER FOOD
Thick crust	Thin crust
⅔ cup sugar	⅔ cup sugar substitute
2 tablespoons butter	No butter
⅔ cup shortening	3 tablespoons light margarine
3 tablespoons flour	1 tablespoon quick-cooking tapioca
Calories per serving: 470	Calories per serving: 160
Fat per serving: 24 g	Fat per serving: 6.5 g

▲ Marble Cheesecake

SERVES 12

The combination of rich taste and creamy texture makes cheesecake one of the most beloved of all desserts. Keep the romance alive by using lighter ingredients.

⅓ cup (85 g/3 oz) low-fat honey graham crackers (6 whole crackers)

½ cup toasted wheat germ

1 tablespoon plus 1 cup sugar

2 tablespoons extra-light olive oil

560 ml (19 oz) (about 2 cups) silken tofu, well drained

450 g (1 lb) fat-free cream cheese

3 tablespoons flour

1 large egg plus 2 large egg whites

1 teaspoon vanilla extract

¼ cup chocolate syrup

1. Preheat the oven to 180˚C (350˚F).

2. Combine the graham crackers, wheat germ, and 1 tablespoon of the sugar in a food processor and process into fine crumbs. Add the oil and process until moistened. Press the mixture into the bottom and partway up the sides of a 23-cm (9-in.) springform pan. Bake until set, about 10 minutes.

3. Add the tofu, cream cheese, flour, egg and egg whites, vanilla, and the remaining 1 cup sugar to the food processor and process until smooth.

4. Measure 1 cup of the tofu mixture into a small bowl and stir in the chocolate syrup. Pour the remaining filling into the crust. Pour the chocolate mixture in a ring on top of the filling and swirl in with a knife. Bake for 45 minutes. Turn off the oven and leave the cheesecake undisturbed for 45 minutes. Cool to room temperature before chilling overnight.

DISASTER FOOD	MASTER FOOD
225 g (8 oz) regular cream cheese	450 g (16 oz) fat-free cream cheese
2 cups regular sour cream	560 ml (about 2 cups) tofu
2 whole eggs	1 whole egg and 2 egg whites
Butter in crust	Olive oil in crust
Calories per serving: 466	Calories per serving: 225
Fat per serving: 34 g	Fat per serving: 5 g

master your disaster foods

▼ Chocolate Mousse

Who would guess that you could have the smooth flavor and texture of this rich dessert with minimal fat and calories? But you can, thanks to sugar-free pudding mix and fat-free whipped topping, which save you a whopping 32 g of fat.

2 cups skim or fat-free milk

1 package sugar-free chocolate instant pudding mix

½ cup (110 g/4 oz) fat-free whipped topping

1. Pour the milk into a medium bowl and add the pudding mix. Stir until dissolved.

2. Stir in the whipped topping.

DISASTER FOOD	MASTER FOOD
2 cups heavy cream	2 cups skim or fat-free milk
110 g (4 oz) semi-sweet chocolate plus ⅔ cup sugar	Sugar-free chocolate pudding mix
4 eggs	No eggs
Whipping cream	Fat-free whipped topping
Calories per serving: 500	Calories per serving: 105
Fat per serving: 32 g	Fat per serving: 0 g

▶TIP To dress up the mousse while adding minimal calories, sprinkle shaved dark chocolate on top or serve with sliced bananas or strawberries.

STEP 5 sensitize with exercise

The Plate Approach will take you a long way toward slimming your waistline, dropping your blood sugar, and possibly even getting you off diabetes medication or lowering your dose. But if you stop there, you're missing out. There's another way to stack the deck in your favor and even help reverse your disease: exercise. It does naturally what some drugs do: Sensitizes cells to insulin so they soak up more glucose from the bloodstream, which brings your blood sugar levels down.

In this step, you'll discover a simple plan to add more exercise to your life 5 minutes at a time.

We'll also provide you with an easy, 10-minute muscle-building workout to boost your metabolism and a relaxing routine to wind down at day's end. You'll see how simple activities—from doing work around the house to tensing your muscles while you sit behind the wheel of your car—can help tone your muscles, burn calories, and bring blood sugar levels closer to normal.

Exercise can make or break your efforts to lose weight and control your blood sugar. The DO IT study—and a long list of other studies over the years—proved it. In one landmark study comparing weight-loss programs using either diet alone, exercise alone, or a combination of both, people who combined approaches lost the most weight after a year. A year after that, those who both ate less and exercised more were still ahead of the diet-only folks, who gained much of their weight back.

It's easy to see why exercise is so important. Let's say you wanted to cut 500 calories a day—about the amount needed to lose 0.5 kg (1 lb) a week. You could eat 500 fewer calories, but if you burned half of those calories by being more active, you'd have to cut only 250 calories from your diet. That would make your eating plan seem a whole lot less stringent.

Exercise also increases your metabolism, so your body uses up more calories even when you're not active. Think of exercising as adding booster rockets to the slow burn of weight loss.

For people with diabetes, though, exercise does much more than aid weight loss. It also sensitizes cells to insulin—in effect, reversing the insulin resistance that is the hallmark of type 2 diabetes. How? When you work your muscles, they become more efficient at using glucose. That's because active muscles demand more energy (in the form of glucose), which forces them to squeeze more glucose out of the blood. This glucose-gobbling effect continues even after you've stopped exercising, lowering your blood sugar for hours after a workout. Also, as your body becomes more conditioned, your toned muscles require more energy all the time, making the glucose-controlling effects of exercise virtually permanent, as long as you stay active. What's more, physical activity also reduces your risk of problems common among people with diabetes, such as high blood pressure, heart attack, stroke, and arthritis.

Once you get going, you'll find that exercise feels so good that you'll want to keep doing it. (Remember, your body was designed to move, not to sit all day.) You'll feel more energetic,

10 Ways to Burn 100 Calories

- 5 minutes of paddling a canoe
- 9 minutes of brisk walking
- 10 minutes of swimming the backstroke
- 12 minutes of playing baseball
- 13 minutes of washing floors
- 14 minutes of playing golf
- 15 minutes of dancing
- 15 minutes of pushing a lawnmower
- 16 minutes of table tennis
- 17 minutes of planting in your garden

sleep better, and even look better. So how do you start? With Action One: Follow the Forward by Five Walking Plan. That's right: When we say "exercise," the main activity we're talking about is taking a sunset jaunt around your neighborhood, orbiting the trail through a local park, or doing some on-the-hoof window shopping at the mall. We're going to ask that you dedicate a certain amount of time on most days to walking—starting with just 10 minutes and adding 5 minutes a week—but you should also take every opportunity to put one foot in front of the other wherever you go.

Once you've gotten into the swing of walking, it will be time to start toning your muscles even more with our oh-so-simple Sugar-Buster Routine. It takes only 10 minutes—and keep in mind that by working your muscles, you're actually helping to reverse your insulin resistance.

Exercise doesn't have to happen just while you're "exercising." It can happen while you're stopped at a red light, standing in line at the post office, or even brushing your teeth. In fact, your day is filled with countless chances to sneak in quickie exercises that tone your muscles and help bring your blood sugar down. Our 30-Second Fitness Boosters are designed to help you make the most of idle time you'd otherwise waste.

Another reason to move your body is to release tension and calm your mind. As you'll learn in Step Six, relaxing is an important way to keep blood sugar under control. That's

Exercise Smarts

Exercise works so well at bringing down your blood sugar that you need to make sure it doesn't drop too low. You'll want to time exercise to your medication or insulin schedule (see page 54), but you should also be prepared to deal with hypoglycemia if it occurs.

- **Know the signs.** Confusion, shaking, lightheadedness, or difficulty speaking all indicate that you should quit exercising immediately.

- **Have a snack handy.** When blood sugar is too low, you can quickly bring it back up with a low-fat, high-carb snack, such as 10 small jelly beans or ½ cup of nondiet soft drink or juice.

- **Use the buddy system.** Try to walk or work out with someone who could lend a hand in an emergency.

- **Carry identification.** Even if you're just strolling through the neighborhood, carry ID with your name, address, and phone number, along with emergency information such as how to reach your doctor and the dosages of your medication or insulin.

because stress hormones directly raise blood sugar—and contribute to weight gain. We've come up with a 10-minute yoga-based program of simple, soothing movements that unclench your muscles and help you rid your body and mind of stress. We call it the Day's-End Wind-Down, but you can do it in the morning or any other time you wish.

Remember to check with your doctor before starting any exercise program, especially if you're over age 35, have had diabetes for more than 10 years, or already show signs of heart disease, poor circulation, or nerve damage. Most people, however, should have no problem with the exercises in this chapter, especially if they start gradually.

ACTION 1: follow the forward by five walking plan

Walking belongs at the core of your activity plan. Why? Because it's an ideal way to get your body moving. Studies find that walking lowers blood sugar even more effectively than other forms of exercise, partly because it engages your muscles for sustained periods of time, which keeps demand for blood glucose high. Just as important, walking is an easy activity that requires no special skills or equipment. You can do it just about anytime, anywhere.

It's true that dedicating yourself to regular walking means that you'll need to make an investment of time. Your goal is to walk at least five days a week. Impossible? Some of the people in the DO IT study thought the same thing—until the weight started melting off and exercise became a priority. You won't get to that point instantly, and we're not asking you to. Instead, you'll build up walking time gradually, in the following way.

START WITH 10 MINUTES

That's about how long it takes to do a single loop around the block—or brew a pot of coffee, browse a magazine, or catch the next local forecast on the Weather Channel. In other words, anyone can carve 10 minutes from a day, yet that's all you need for starters.

For five days during the first week, do nothing but your 10-minute walks. Once you get going, you'll be surprised how quickly your walks become a habit. That's not as glib as it may sound. We realize that the simple act of going outside to get some exercise may seem like a big change. In fact, the toughest part may be taking that first step out the door, so start with that: Just open the door and walk outside as if you were getting the morning paper. Next, walk to the end of the driveway as if you were getting the mail. Then steer yourself to the end of the block as if you'd seen a neighbor you'd like to chat with. Keep moving forward in small steps like that, and you'll have walked 10 minutes in no time.

The next thing you know, you may even start looking forward to getting out. Think of all that awaits you: fresh air, time away from your responsibilities, and a chance to see what's going on around the neighborhood (believe us, you'll notice things you would have overlooked zooming by in a car).

MOVE **FORWARD BY 5** MINUTES EACH WEEK

Five more minutes a day is not a lot to ask, and it may not seem like a big improvement in the amount of exercise you do. In fact, that's the point. By moving forward by 5 minutes each week, you'll add to your walking almost imperceptibly, so it never seems like a big deal. Nevertheless, those minutes add up and can make a significant impact on your blood sugar. After all, 5 more minutes on five days amounts to 25 minutes of extra walking time per week.

Pick an official starting day for your walking week—most people choose Sunday or Monday—and tack on 5 minutes of walking that day, then try to stick to your new routine until you move forward by another 5. How long should this continue? Aim to build up to at least 45 minutes a day. If you start with 10 minutes and stay on track, that will take you eight weeks. Even before you reach that mark, though, you'll trim weight from your body, and maintaining that routine will keep the weight off. Want to continue improving after your eight weeks are up? Crank up the intensity by walking faster or more often.

TAKE A DAY TO REASSESS

One day a week, preferably in the middle of your weekly walking cycle, check in with yourself. Your physical condition

Steps to Success

Maria Holland, a 34-year-old participant in the DO IT study, remembers the moment she realized what exercise could do to bring down her blood sugar. "One night after dinner, I tested my blood sugar and it was 12," she says. "Then I went for a 20-minute walk and took a reading again, and my sugars were down to 7. I'd never done a before-and-after comparison before, and it was a real eye-opener to see how big a difference I could make just by walking."

That was incentive enough to make 20-minute walks part of her routine just about every day. "I felt I could start with 20 minutes," she says. "I was capable of exercise, but until then, I just didn't do it." Two weeks into her walking routine, however, she started to feel a definite change of attitude. "Exercise is one of those things you don't always feel like doing, but if you do it anyway, you feel good afterward," she says. "I started to feel like I wanted to do more." By the third or fourth week, "I became almost addicted to it," she says. "If I didn't go out for a walk, it just felt wrong." Holland quickly worked up to 30-minute walks and would even go as long as an hour if she had the time. Blessed with a safe neighborhood, she would often take peaceful, quiet jaunts through residential streets at night.

Just as important, Holland started finding ways to work more steps into her day. At the hospital where she worked as a nurse, for example, she'd take the stairs if she had to climb three flights or less. At home, she took over mowing the lawn from her husband. And whenever she took one of her children, ages 14, 12, and 3, to soccer or baseball practice, she'd walk the perimeter of the field instead of sitting and waiting.

Within two months, Holland's blood sugar dropped to normal levels—something medication had been unable to accomplish before she exercised—and she dropped 30 kg (65 lb) during the study. Since then, she's lost 14 kg (30 lb) more. Part of the secret, she says, is that walking helps her stick to her eating plan. "If I eat a cupcake, I think of all the exercise it would take to burn it off," she says. "It's a mindset you get into that keeps you motivated."

and capabilities are different from everybody else's, so this is a chance to decide whether you should make any adjustments to your program. Ask yourself the following questions.

- Is it hard to get motivated to walk because the effort seems daunting?
- Do I feel tired after I finish a walk?
- Does walking cause any kind of pain?
- Do I feel invigorated and full of energy?
- Does the amount I'm walking seem tame?
- Am I free from uncomfortable soreness or any damage to my feet?

If you answer yes to any of the first three questions, especially if you're clinically obese, trim today's walk back by 5 minutes. If exercise feels punishing, you're not likely to stick with it, so don't feel you have to push yourself beyond what you—or your body—are ready for. Maybe you're just tired today. Tomorrow, go back to this week's walking time. If you still feel fatigued and sluggish then, stick with 5 fewer minutes for the rest of this week. When you feel comfortable adding another 5 minutes, proceed with the plan.

If you answer yes to any of the last three questions, add another 5 minutes to your walk today—you're clearly capable of more, and this is a chance to push yourself. Tomorrow, either stick with the new time goal or revert to the week's original plan—the choice is yours.

BUILD IN **WILD CARD** DAYS

Our program calls for you to walk five days a week. What do you do on the other days? Anything but nothing. Don't think of "off" days as vacations from activity. Instead, think of them as Wild Card days, when anything goes—as long as it's your body that's doing the going. Want to get in some more walking? Go ahead! Prefer to skip the walking and work up a sweat in your garden instead? Be our guest. Did you kick a ball with your grandchild for 20 minutes, then walk home from the playground? Chalk it up as your exercise for the day. Wild Card days are also perfect for hobbies such as golf or tennis (and a good reason to take up a new hobby—ballroom dance class anyone?).

STEP UP YOUR EFFORTS

Don't think of your Forward by Five walks as the only movement you need to do all day. Once upon a time, people walked almost everywhere they needed to go, and daily life is still filled with opportunities to power yourself to your destination, whether it's the second floor of a mall (take the stairs, not the escalator) or a mailbox down the street. Every step you take, whether or not you're consciously exercising, burns calories. Be intentional about taking more of them, even when you're not on one of your walks.

One way to do it: When your regular walking hits the 30-minute mark, buy a pedometer, a small device you wear on your waist that counts each step you take. The number of steps you take in a given amount of time varies according to the length of your stride, but your numbers will already be well in the thousands if you're walking 30 minutes a day. Build on that by trying to hit a higher mark. If you're at 8,500 steps a day, for example, aim for 9,000. Work toward the milestone of 10,000 steps a day. Even if nobody's counting, walk more every chance you get.

If you've spent your life looking for ways to save steps, it may be tough to reverse all that mental conditioning and think of ways to, in effect, become less efficient. But those small losses in efficiency add up to gains that speed your efforts to get your blood sugar in line—and there's nothing inefficient about that. Here are eight ways to "step up" to the plate.

- If you're meeting a friend, catch up over a stroll instead of a cup of coffee (or order coffee to go).
- Have a cell phone? Walk while you talk. They don't call them mobile phones for nothing!

Help!

I know exercise helps me, but I just can't get motivated to go out the door for a walk.

Call it the threshold barrier: Taking that first step is always the hardest. Sometimes, with life so busy, you just don't think to exercise. Other times, you know you should but lack the gumption. Here are some steps that can help.

- Put your favorite walking shoes by the door at night so you'll see them first thing in the morning. They'll remind you that getting out there is a priority.

- Have a destination in mind. Going to the store, post office, newsstand, or coffee house makes walking seem more purposeful and time-worthy.

- Book walking time on your calendar. Once you've booked the time, post adhesive reminder notes on the fridge and doors to spur you on—a technique shown to work in studies.

- Enlist a friend to walk with you or, if that's not possible, to call and ask if you've walked. A sense of accountability is one of the best motivators for exercise.

- Find an article of clothing that fit when you weighed 10 percent less or a photo of yourself at the time. Place it on your dresser as an inspirational reminder of your goal.

- Running an errand nearby? Get on your feet instead of in the car.
- In airports, walk around the terminal while waiting for your flight—and avoid the moving sidewalks.
- During TV commercials, walk in place, climb up and down the stairs, or take a spin around the perimeter of the house.
- Don't fight for parking. Avoid the aggravation of jockeying for a space close to the door and park farther away.
- Return your shopping cart to the front of the store instead of leaving it in the parking lot.
- Instead of using the drive-through, go inside.

ACTION 2 add a sugar-buster routine

Walking is aerobic exercise—that is, it's sustained over a period of time, so it gets your heart and lungs working and builds endurance. It's a great start, but it's not the only kind of exercise you can—or should—be doing to beat diabetes. Building strength is important, too. Why bother building stronger muscles? The reason is simple: Even when you're not exercising, bigger, denser muscles need more energy, which means they burn more calories and siphon more glucose out of your blood. Imagine: You can beat back diabetes just by sitting still—as long as you keep your muscles in shape.

The investment you need to make to get those results may not be as great as you think. The routine that we've designed, starting on page 144, can be done in 10 minutes—roughly the time you'd spend watching commercials during a typical half-hour TV show—so it's easy to do this workout during your favorite program. If you've never done strength exercises before (or simply don't enjoy them very much), we've broken the workout into sequences that take only 2 to 3 minutes and don't have to be done at the same time. Consider the advantages of exercising in 2-minute sequences.

- You can fit strength exercise into any schedule. For example, you can do one sequence in the morning, another at noon, and the third in the late afternoon. You can do one sequence on different days of the week so you develop a habit of doing a little exercise almost every day. Or, of course, you can do the entire workout at once.

Protecting Your Feet

Walking is one of the safest forms of exercise, but when you have diabetes, complications such as nerve damage and impaired circulation can put your feet at risk for serious damage. You shouldn't avoid walking, but you should take the following precautions to keep your feet healthy.

- Check your feet every day. If you have nerve damage, you could have sores, cuts, swelling, or infection that you can't feel.

- Avoid cracked skin and reduce the risk of infection by toweling your feet off thoroughly after bathing, especially between your toes. Rub lotion or cream on the tops and bottoms of your feet to keep them moist, and sprinkle talcum powder or cornstarch between your toes to prevent fungal growth.

- Trim your toenails at least once a week after bathing, cutting straight across the nails and smoothing them with a nail file or emery board.

- Always wear socks and shoes. Socks should be seamless to avoid pressure points and friction, and shoes are best made of leather, which conforms to your feet and breathes to keep them drier.

- To boost blood circulation to your feet, wiggle your toes for 5 minutes two or three times a day. Avoid tight elastic socks, don't cross your legs for long periods of time, and put your feet up when you're sitting.

- You never exercise so hard that you work up a sweat, so you can do the exercises at any time and in any type of clothing.

- You can squeeze exercise into small bits of time, such as the moments between finishing getting dressed in the morning and going downstairs for breakfast, or the time between getting home from work and sitting down to dinner.

THE **SUGAR-BUSTER** ROUTINE

Both efficient and effective, this workout uses exercises that work more than one major muscle group at once, saving you time and effort. Some exercises (such as the slow hundred) draw on the torso-strengthening methods of Pilates, while others (such as the airplane pose) are adapted from yoga. All are basic exercises that will come easily to people at any level of ability. Here are some guidelines to get you started.

STICK TO SEQUENCES. The routine is divided into three sequences. Do just one sequence if you're short on time or energy, or do the whole routine at once.

- **Upper Body** works the chest, triceps, and shoulders.
- **Lower Body** targets the hamstrings and quadriceps.
- **Core Body** strengthens the abdominals and lower back.

ESTABLISH A SCHEDULE. Introduce the exercises gradually

Sample Activity Schedule

Here's an example of how your Forward by Five walking plan might play out over the course of eight weeks. Remember, if you find the plan too easy, feel free to add more minutes. Use your Wild Card days to substitute any physical activity you want, from playing ball with the kids to raking the yard, for walking. We've

	WEEK 1 GET OUT THE DOOR!	WEEK 2 BUILD ON YOUR NEW HABIT	WEEK 3 TAKE YOURSELF TO A NEW DESTINATION	WEEK 4 EASE INTO THE SUGAR-BUSTER ROUTINE
MON	10-minute walk	15-minute walk	20-minute walk	25-minute walk Sugar Buster: Upper Body
TUES	10-minute walk	15-minute walk	20-minute walk	25-minute walk
WED	Assessment day: 5- or 15-minute walk	Assessment day: 10- or 20-minute walk	Assessment day: 15- or 25-minute walk	Assessment day: 20- or 30-minute walk
THUR	10-minute walk	15-minute walk	20-minute walk	25-minute walk Sugar Buster: Lower Body
FRI	*Wild Card day*	*Wild Card day*	*Wild Card day*	*Wild Card day*
SAT	10-minute walk	15-minute walk	20-minute walk	25-minute walk Sugar Buster: Core Body
SUN	*Wild Card day*	*Wild Card day*	*Wild Card day*	*Wild Card day*

(doing just one a day is a good way to start), but aim to eventually do the entire program at least twice a week. The simplest schedule is to do the entire workout on two different days, or you can continue to do one sequence a day.

also indicated where you might fit in your Sugar-Buster Routine. Need to move the days around? No problem—but be sure to decide on a schedule *before* you start, then post it on your refrigerator or write it in your calendar. Committing to a schedule greatly increases your chances of carrying through.

	WEEK 5	WEEK 6	WEEK 7	WEEK 8
	KEEP ON TRUCKING!	**COMBINE THE SUGAR-BUSTER SEGMENTS**	**YOUR BODY IS LOOKING BETTER**	**GREAT JOB! NOW KEEP UP THE GOOD WORK**
MON	30-minute walk **Sugar Buster: Upper Body**	35-minute walk **Sugar-Buster Routine**	40-minute walk **Sugar-Buster Routine**	45-minute walk **Sugar-Buster Routine**
TUES	30-minute walk	35-minute walk	40-minute walk	45-minute walk
WED	Assessment day: 25- or 35-minute walk	Assessment day: 30- or 40-minute walk	Assessment day: 35- or 45-minute walk	Assessment day: 40- or 50-minute walk
THUR	30-minute walk **Sugar Buster: Lower Body**	35-minute walk **Sugar-Buster Routine**	40-minute walk **Sugar-Buster Routine**	45-minute walk **Sugar-Buster Routine**
FRI	*Wild Card day*	*Wild Card day*	*Wild Card day*	*Wild Card day*
SAT	30-minute walk **Sugar Buster: Core Body**	35-minute walk **Sugar-Buster Routine**	40-minute walk **Sugar-Buster Routine**	45-minute walk **Sugar-Buster Routine**
SUN	*Wild Card day*	*Wild Card day*	*Wild Card day*	*Wild Card day*

3 ACTION

sneak in stealthy exercise

What kind of exercise can you do while stuck in a line at the grocery store? The kind you can do with a smile on your face—because if people realized you were working your butt muscles, inquiring minds might find you more interesting than the tabloid headlines. Our 30-Second Fitness Boosters starting on page 152 will not only build your body, they'll also keep your thoughts occupied—not a bad thing if you'd otherwise ponder how delicious a candy bar from the checkout rack would taste right now.

Most of us hate to kill time, but we face countless opportunities during the day to do just that. Opportunities? That's right: From now on, be alert for small moments of downtime during your day and wait for them with anticipation, because they're perfect chances to build some extra exercise into your day. You can do some of the 30-Second Fitness Boosters while standing in line at the bank, sitting in traffic, or cooling your heels while waiting at the assigned time and place for friends or family members (who apparently don't know how to tell time). Others you can do in the privacy of your home while

8 Ways to Burn Calories without Noticing

1. Take the escalator—but climb the stairs while you ride. You'll get there faster and use your muscles while you're at it. Just 5 minutes of stair climbing burns 144 calories.

2. Instead of piling items on stairs so you can take all of them upstairs at once, take them one at a time.

3. When cooling your heels while waiting in a doctor's office, drugstore, or airport, stay on your feet—standing burns 36 more calories per hour than sitting.

4. Rake leaves instead of using a leaf blower: You'll burn 50 more calories every half hour.

5. Scrub your floors more often. Putting some elbow grease into cleaning floors is more intense exercise than vacuuming—and it makes your floors look better to boot.

6. Chew sugarless gum. Research has found that the action of jaw muscles alone burns about 11 calories an hour.

7. Wash your car by hand instead of taking it through the automatic carwash. You'll burn an extra 280 calories in an hour.

8. Play with kids: Impromptu games of basketball, touch football, or tag—or just jumping rope or throwing a ball—will help you use energy and set a good example of active play for the children. Calories burned: 80 to 137 every 10 minutes.

Analyzing Your Activity

It's easy to let false assumptions or lack of time get in the way of being more active. For a sense of how to deal with obstacles to exercise, answer the following questions.

1. Check each statement about lifestyle that's true for you:
- ❑ I do yard work such as pushing a lawnmower or gardening for at least an hour a week.
- ❑ I do moderately vigorous house-work such as scrubbing the floor or cleaning windows for a total of at least an hour a week.
- ❑ I make a habit of taking stairs instead of elevators.
- ❑ In my job, I often walk or move around.

2. Check each statement about exercise that's true for you:
- ❑ I walk, play tennis, or ride a bike for at least 40 minutes a week.
- ❑ I walk once in a while.
- ❑ The only exercise I get is looking for the remote control.

3. The best exercise for losing weight is:
- ❑ Running.
- ❑ Walking.
- ❑ Swimming.
- ❑ Biking.

4. Which of the following do you think will burn more calories?
- ❑ Walking through the neighborhood for 10 minutes after breakfast and 10 minutes after dinner.
- ❑ Strolling an extra 2 minutes to and from your car on five trips to the store.
- ❑ Walking 20 minutes in the mall.

5. Check any of the following statements that reflect your feelings or beliefs:
- ❑ Exercise will just make me hungry, and I'll eat more.
- ❑ I don't like to sweat.
- ❑ I have no energy for exercise.
- ❑ I'm just not an exercise person.

6. When I'm feeling tired, I:
- ❑ Plop down in front of the TV.
- ❑ Reach for a candy bar.
- ❑ Take a brisk 10-minute walk.

7. For each amount of time, list an activity you normally do each day that you could eliminate without major consequences:

3 minutes: _____
_____

10 minutes: _____
_____

20 minutes: _____
_____

30 minutes: _____
_____

8. My favorite physical activities are:
- ❑ Shooting hoops, playing Frisbee, or throwing a ball.
- ❑ Walking my dog.
- ❑ Working around the house.
- ❑ Shopping.
- ❑ Other _____
_____
_____

Turn the page to evaluate your answers.

quiz
What Your Score Means

1. If you checked any of these, great! You're already working physical activity into every week. Don't rest on your laurels, though: Several of these would need to be true to turn the tables on your weight. Our exercise program will help you build more movement into your life—which is especially critical if you didn't check any answers here.

2. If you checked the first answer, congratulations! You're well on your way to getting in shape, which will lengthen your life expectancy. If you checked the second answer, it must mean you like walking, so you'll do fine on the Forward by Five Walking Plan. If you checked the last answer, pay special attention to the advice in this step: It will get you going again.

3. These will all help you lose weight—but only if you stick with them. Since studies find that people are more likely to stick with walking than with other exercise routines, we made walking the basis of our Forward by Five plan.

4. All of these burn the same number of calories, which shows how easy it is to work more activity into your life, no matter what your schedule.

5. If you didn't check any boxes, great! If you did, don't let excuses like these stop you from exercising. Studies find that moderate exercise doesn't stimulate your appetite. None of the exercises in our program are so intense that you'll sweat a lot. Moving your body will boost your energy, not drain it. And you don't have to be an "exercise person"—you just have to be more active.

6. Plopping down on the couch won't do much to help—but the walk will. A brisk 10-minute walk can give you more energy than eating a candy bar—a 1997 study proved it. Exercise boosts a hormone that increases energy. In this step, you'll find plenty of ways to fit quick bursts of activity into your day.

7. Have 3 minutes to spare? You can do one of the sequences from our Sugar-Buster Routine. Have 10 minutes? You can do the whole routine or the Day's-End Wind-Down. Have 30 minutes? That's plenty of time for a walk on the Forward by Five plan.

8. The cardinal rule for making your life more active is to do what you like. Find a physical activity that you enjoy, then do it more often.

you go about everyday activities, such as brushing your teeth or heating a pot of water for tea.

ACTION 4 do the day's-end wind-down

....

After a long day, doing more exercise may be the last thing on your mind. But our yoga-based routine isn't so much about exercise as about stretching and relaxing or refreshing—perfect for either evening or morning. Yoga is famous for relieving stress, promoting health, and making muscles more flexible—an element of fitness that's frequently overlooked but essential for increasing mobility, relieving stiffness, and promoting a sense of well-being. This routine, starting on page 162, may even help keep your blood sugar down and dampen a rise in glucose that many people with diabetes experience in the morning. How? By lowering your levels of stress hormones. (You'll read more about this in Step Six.)

You don't have to study with a guru or even take a class to begin putting yoga-based moves to work: The poses and movements in the Day's-End Wind-Down are simple. Perform them in the order we've suggested so that each exercise leads straight into the next. Once you become familiar with the routine, don't pause between movements; just let the entire workout flow until you reach the end, which should take only about 10 minutes. Don't be in a rush to finish, though: The idea is to get off life's roller coaster and relax.

While moving through the exercises, breathe evenly and deliberately and coordinate your movements with your breathing (we'll tell you when to breathe in and out). The more automatic the routine becomes, the easier it will be to let your mind go, which is an important part of relaxing.

If you're like many people, you may discover that you're not very flexible. Take heart: The more often you do this routine, the more limber you'll become.

*Y*ou can perform the entire Sugar-Buster Routine in about 10 minutes, so there are no excuses for not fitting it in. To make strength training even easier to swallow, do just the Upper Body sequence, the Lower Body sequence, or the Core Body sequence, then do a different sequence tomorrow. Each of them takes just 3 minutes.

▶ Upper Body

Wall Push

Stand facing a wall about an arm's length away, with your feet directly under your hips. Lean forward and place your palms against the wall with your elbows slightly bent. **1**

Inhale as you slowly bend your elbows, bringing your chest closer to the wall. **2** Exhale and slowly press back to the starting position. Do 15 times.

▶**BENEFIT** Strengthens the chest and triceps muscles in a single movement.

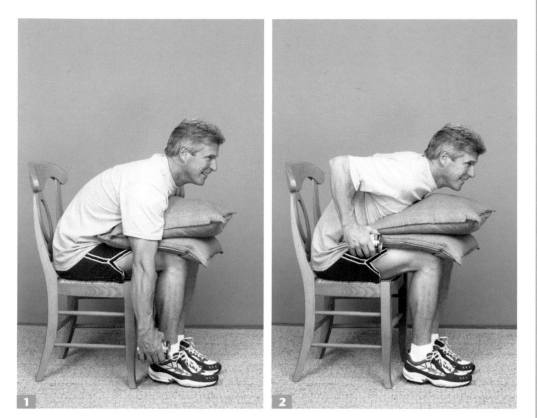

Bent-Arm Row

Sit in a hard-back chair with a large pillow on your lap for support.
Grasping a full soup can or a light hand weight in each hand, lean forward, keeping your back as straight as possible. Let your hands hang
toward the floor. **1**

Exhale as you raise your elbows toward the ceiling, keeping them close
to your body. **2** Hold for 1 second, then inhale as you return to the
starting position. Do 10 times.

▶**BENEFIT** Works the middle and upper back and, to a lesser extent, the biceps.

Airplane

Stand with your feet hip-width apart. **1** (If it's more comfortable, you can do this exercise while seated.)

Exhale and raise your arms straight out to the sides, with your palms facing down and your fingers open and relaxed, until your hands reach shoulder height. **2** Don't lock your elbows. Hold for 60 seconds, breathing normally, then lower your arms. Do one time.

▶**BENEFIT** Works all three sections of the shoulder muscles, which helps maintain an erect upper-body posture. To increase intensity, hold a small full soup can in each hand.

▶ Lower Body

Wall Slide with Raised Arms

Stand with your back pressed firmly against a wall from your shoulders to your tailbone. Keeping your back in contact with the wall, move your feet forward about 1 foot. **1**

Breathe in and slide your back down the wall until your knees are bent at a 90-degree angle (or as far as is comfortable) while simultaneously raising your arms in front of you to shoulder height. **2** Hold this position for as long as is comfortable. When your legs start to feel warm, breathe in and slide back up the wall while lowering your arms to your sides. Do four times.

▶**BENEFIT** Strengthens the shoulders and works the large muscles of the hips and buttocks for improved walking performance. To increase intensity, hold a small full soup can in each hand.

Lift Pump

Stand 30 cm (12 in.) from a wall with your feet hip-width apart. Place your hands on the wall for support, but don't lean into it. **1**

Exhaling, lift your right leg toward your buttocks, stopping when your knee is bent at a 90-degree angle. **2** Hold for 10 seconds. Do five times with each leg.

▶**BENEFIT** Works the hamstring muscles at the back of the upper leg. To increase intensity, put two full soup cans in a pair of socks, tie the socks together, and drape them over the back of your ankle as you lift your leg.

▶ Core Body

Dry Swimming

Lie facedown on a mat or rug with your arms and legs stretched out straight, like Superman in flight. **1**

Keeping your neck relaxed (don't lift your head), tense your abdominal muscles, then raise your right arm and left leg and hold for 1 second. **2** Slowly lower both limbs and repeat with the other arm and leg. "Swim" for 30 seconds.

▶**BENEFIT** Strengthens the lower back and bolsters the muscles that run along the lower part of the spine, improving posture and preventing lower-back pain.

Baby Lift

Lie on your back with your knees bent, your feet flat on the floor, and your hands behind your head, with your elbows out to the sides. **1**

Inhale and contract your abdominal muscles so your lower back makes contact with the floor, then raise your right foot about 3 cm (1 in.) off the floor. **2** Hold for a count of 4, then exhale while lowering your foot to the floor to a count of 4. Repeat with the left leg.

▶**BENEFIT** Like a traditional crunch, this exercise works the abdominal muscles, but it's less intense and doesn't require you to lift your head off the floor, which can strain your neck.

Slow Hundred

Lie on your back with your legs together and your knees bent at a 90-degree angle. Inhale and raise your arms toward the ceiling without raising your shoulders off the floor. **1**

Exhaling, curl your torso up so the tops of your shoulders come off the floor. At the same time, lower your arms to your sides and hold them at hip height. **2**

Contracting your abdominal muscles, pump your arms up and down (imagine you're using a bicycle pump), counting each pump until you reach 100.

▶**BENEFIT** Strengthens the "core" muscles: the abdominals, the lower-back muscles, and the muscles attached to the spine.

*E*ven *as you go through your usual routine, you can add more movement to your day. Do one of these 30-Second Fitness Boosters while you're brushing your teeth, sitting in the car, standing in line, sitting at your desk, or waiting for water to boil.*

▶ At the sink

Tree Pose

Stand up straight with your legs together. Slowly raise your left knee to the side, resting the bottom of your left foot against the inner calf of your right leg. Balance there for a count of 15, keeping your right knee unlocked. Pull your stomach in for support and keep your back straight and your chin up. Repeat on the other side.

▶**BENEFIT** Strengthens the lower body and core support muscles of the lower back and abdomen.

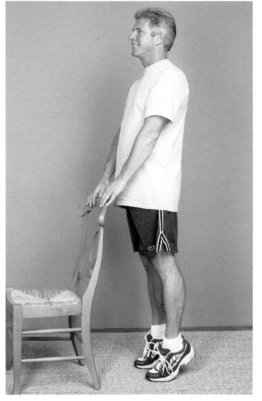

Calf Raise

Stand with your feet directly under your hips, with your arms resting comfortably at your sides or your hands on the sink if you need help with balance. Slowly rise on your toes and hold for 30 seconds, then slowly lower yourself back down. Do three times.

▶**BENEFIT** Strengthens the calves and shins, which improves agility and balance and helps you push off with your toes when walking.

▶ In the car

Steering Wheel Lift Press

While stopped at a red light, grasp the bottom of the steering wheel with your palms up. Inhale and then, while exhaling, push up on the wheel with your palms as hard as you can. Hold while breathing normally until the light turns green.

▶**BENEFIT** Works the biceps, the primary load-bearing muscles of the arms.

Ab Squeeze

While stopped at a red light or stop sign, take a deep breath through your mouth, dropping your diaphragm so your stomach pushes out. While exhaling, squeeze your abdominal muscles so your back presses into the car seat. (Imagine that a hook around your spine is pulling you back.) Hold for up to 60 seconds while breathing normally.

▶**BENEFIT** Improves posture and tones the gut to support your back and make you look slimmer.

▶ Standing in line

Standing Ab Squeeze

Stand with your feet hip-width apart. **1** Keeping your neck, shoulders, and arms relaxed, pull in and tighten the muscles of your abdomen. (Picture a belt being tightened around your midsection.) **2** Hold for 60 seconds, breathing normally. Do three times.

▶**BENEFIT** Doing this exercise while standing strengthens muscles that support your back against the strain of extra weight in your gut.

Butt Buster

Stand up straight with your feet hip-width apart, your arms at your sides, and your shoulders relaxed. Squeeze the muscles of your buttocks together as tightly as you can, hold in your stomach, and move your right leg about 5 cm (2 in.) behind you with your foot off the floor. Hold for 10 seconds, then switch legs. Do at least three times with each leg.

▶**BENEFIT** Strengthens the humble but powerful muscles in your buttocks, which are involved in virtually every movement your body makes.

▶ At your desk

Upper Back Push-Down

Sit at your desk, preferably in a chair without wheels. Position the chair 60 to 90 cm (2 to 3 ft) from the desk and keep your feet flat on the floor. Inhale and bend forward, extending your arms straight onto the desktop with your palms down and your fingers spread apart. Exhale and press down with your hands and forearms as hard as you can. Hold for 30 seconds. Do four times.

▶BENEFIT Strengthens the lower body and core support muscles of the lower back and abdomen.

Overhead Press

Sit up straight with your back firmly against the back of your chair
and your feet flat on the floor, about hip-width apart. Raise your arms
over your head with your palms flat and your elbows facing to the sides.
Inhale and press up as if you were going to push the ceiling with your
hands. Hold for 30 seconds, breathing normally. Repeat.

▶**BENEFIT** The palm position of this exercise isolates and strengthens the muscles
of the shoulders.

Thigh Toner

Sit up straight. While tucking in your stomach muscles, curl your hands into fists and place them between your knees. Squeeze your fists with your thighs and hold for 30 seconds. Repeat.

▶**BENEFIT** Strengthens and firms the difficult-to-isolate muscles of the inner thighs.

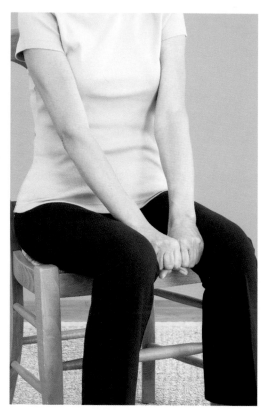

Palm Clasp

Sit up straight and grab one hand with the other. Press your palms together hard for 5 seconds, then release. Do four times. You can also do this one at red lights or while watching TV.

▶**BENEFIT** This anytime-anywhere exercise strengthens the chest and arms.

▶In the kitchen

Knee Raise

While waiting for water to boil, stand sideways near the counter. Place your left hand on the counter for balance. **1**

Transfer all your weight to your left leg and raise your right knee to hip level. **2** Hold for 5 seconds, return your foot to the floor, and repeat with the other leg. Do five times with each leg.

▶**BENEFIT** Strengthens the thighs, hamstrings, and hip extensor muscles. Working your leg muscles supports your knee, which allows it to better absorb impact while walking.

Triceps Kickback

Stand with your feet hip-width apart, your back straight, and your knees flexed. Grasp a full small soup can (no more than 284 ml) in each hand and rest them against the sides of your thighs. **1**

Keeping your elbows and wrists fixed, exhale and raise the cans behind you as far as is comfortable. **2** Hold for 5 seconds. Inhale and return to the starting position. Do five times.

▶**BENEFIT** Works the triceps, which are important for pushing, such as moving a heavy shopping cart, and lifting, such as carrying grocery bags from the car. Tones away that "jiggly" appearance.

Biceps Curl

Stand with your feet shoulder-width apart, holding a full soup can in each hand by your sides, palms facing forward. **1**

Exhaling, curl your forearms toward your chest, keeping your elbows close to your sides. **2** Keep your abdominal muscles tensed and don't allow your lower back to sway. Hold for 1 second. Inhale and return to the starting position. Do five times.

▶**BENEFIT** Works the biceps, which are important for pulling, such as yanking weeds in the garden, and lifting, whether it's a grocery bag or a grandchild.

This yoga-based routine stretches out the kinks and moves the blood through your body. It works as a morning wake-up routine, too. Do the whole routine, and don't pause between movements. You'll get more flexible the more you practice this.

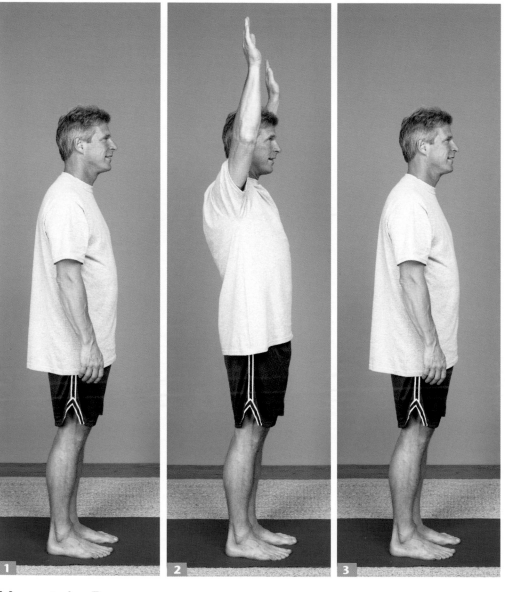

Mountain Pose

Stand with your feet hip-width apart. **1**

Inhaling, slowly raise your arms to the sides and continue until they are over your head, with your palms facing forward. **2**

Exhaling, slowly lower your arms. **3** Repeat.

Standing Forward Bend

Inhale and repeat the mountain pose so that your arms are extended above your head, palms facing forward. **4**

Exhaling, bend forward at the waist, keeping a slight bend in your elbows and knees. **5** Try to touch the floor or your ankles or shins, depending on what's comfortable. Roll back up to the starting position. Repeat.

▶ **CAUTION** If you have back pain, place a small stool or a stack of books about 30 cm (12 in.) high by your feet and reach toward that.

Triangle Pose

Stand with your feet 60 to 90 cm (2 to 3 ft) apart (wider than hip-width), with your toes facing forward.

Inhaling, raise your arms to the sides until they reach shoulder level, palms down, so your upper body forms a T. **6**

Exhaling, bend forward at the waist and reach with your left hand toward your right ankle, foot, or calf (whichever feels most comfortable), placing your right hand on the small of your back. **7** Return to the T position and repeat on the other side. **8** Do three times.

Standing Side Stretch

Stand with your feet 60 to 90 cm (2 to 3 ft) apart (wider than hip-width) and raise your arms to the sides to form a T. **9**

Exhaling, bend to the right and grasp your right leg with right your hand just below the knee while bending your left arm slightly so your left hand moves closer to your ear. **10**

Inhaling, return to the starting position and repeat on the other side. **11** Do three times.

Touchdown Tilt

Lie on your back with your knees bent and about hip-width apart, with your arms at your sides and your hands on the floor, palms down. **12**

Inhaling, raise your hands over your head as if you were a football referee signaling a touchdown. **13** Let your back arch slightly and touch your hands to the floor above your head or, if it's more comfortable, rest them by your ears with your elbows bent.

Exhaling, bring your arms back to your sides and flatten your back gently toward the floor. Do three times.

Lying Twist

Lie on your back with your right knee bent so your foot is on the floor near your left knee. **14**

Exhaling, turn your head to the right and use your left hand to gently pull your right knee toward the floor on the left. **15**

Inhale and return to the starting position. Repeat on the other side. Do three times.

Upward Raised Legs

Lie on your back and use your hands to pull your knees toward your chest, keeping them slightly apart. **16**

Inhaling, extend your legs straight up from your hips so the bottoms of your feet point toward the ceiling. At the same time, extend your arms above your head in the "touchdown" position, keeping your chin tucked into your chest. (Place a small pillow under your head if it's more comfortable.) **17**

Exhaling, return to the starting position. Do three times.

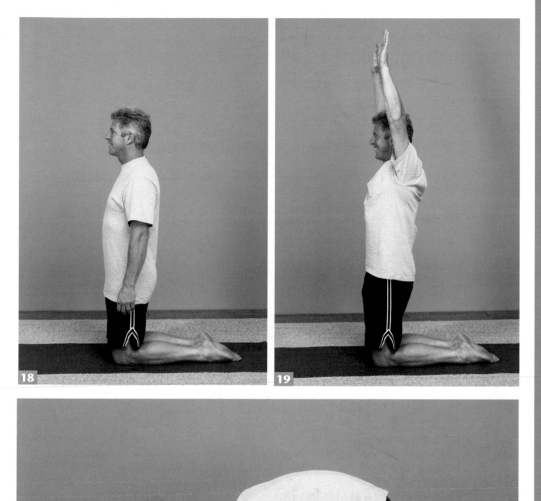

Relaxation Pose

Kneel on a rug or mat with your knees slightly apart and your arms at your sides. **18**

Inhaling, raise your arms straight over your head. (If that's uncomfortable, raise your arms in front of you at a 45-degree angle.) **19**

Exhaling, bend forward at the waist and lower your extended hands and forearms to the floor, moving your hips back so you're sitting on your feet. **20** Hold for 30 to 60 seconds. Do one time.

Cat Pose

From the relaxation pose, get on your hands and knees. Inhaling and keeping your weight distributed evenly on your arms and legs, raise your chin and let your back arch so it makes a gentle U-shaped dip toward the floor. **21**

Exhaling, move your hips back, lower your head, and tilt your pelvis to round your spine, starting with your lower back and progressing through your middle and upper back. **22** At the end of the pose, your head should be slightly lower than your hips. Do three times.

Kneeling Rest Pose

From the cat pose, lower your hips until you're in a kneeling position. Keeping your back straight, rest your hands lightly on your thighs. **23** Close your eyes and breathe slowly for 1 minute.

If this position is uncomfortable for you, try placing a pillow between your feet and your buttocks.

STEP **6** master your **moods**

Calm down. Relax. Take it easy. That's what we want you to do next. Think that sounds like slacking off? Nothing could be further from the truth. Counteracting the stresses, strains, and irritations of daily life can make your body handle blood sugar better and even help you store less abdominal fat. Lowering your body's levels of so-called stress hormones will even make you less hungry.

Dedicated relaxation is part of the 10 Percent Plan. In fact, we want you to set aside 20 minutes a day to purposefully unwind.

From deep breathing drills to exercises using your imagination, there are plenty of ways in this chapter to spend those 20 minutes. Beyond them, treat yourself to an occasional massage—it could actually lower your blood sugar—and employ another powerful blood sugar–lowering weapon: sleep. All of these approaches will help you stick to your goals and focus on a truly important aspect of your life: your health.

The Reason to Relax

Eating right and getting your body in motion every day are pillars of any program for managing diabetes or losing weight. The 10 Percent Plan brings in a third element that may be almost as important: getting a handle on stress.

Research is now beginning to reveal just how important stress management is when it comes to diabetes. One study, at Duke University in Durham, North Carolina, found that when people used easy relaxation techniques like the ones you'll learn here, they dropped their A1C numbers (an indication of blood sugar levels over a period of several months) significantly. In fact, about a third of the volunteers lowered their A1C levels by 1 percent or more after a year—an effect on a par with that of diabetes drugs. And those results were *beyond* what they gained through diet and exercise.

Track Your Sugar Trends

Studies find that stress affects blood sugar differently from one person to the next. How do your sugar levels change when you're all charged up? To find out, each time you check your glucose level, rate how stressed you feel at that moment on a scale of 1 to 10, with 1 being a sunny day at the beach and 10 being the worst day of your life. Write the number down next to your reading. After two weeks, look at the numbers together (plotting them on a graph can help) to see how much your blood sugar swings in response to various levels of stress.

STRESS HORMONES RAISE BLOOD SUGAR. Why does taming tension bring blood sugar down? A number of factors appear to be at work. First, when you're on edge, your body pumps out stress hormones, such as cortisol, to help you react to danger (part of the "fight or flight" response). Among other things, these hormones make your heartbeat and breathing speed up. They also send glucose stores into the blood to make energy immediately available to your muscles. The result: higher blood sugar.

STRESS CONTRIBUTES TO INSULIN RESISTANCE. That's bad enough when you have diabetes, but there's more: Stress hormones also make it more difficult for the pancreas to secrete the insulin that's needed to move glucose out of the blood. Some of these hormones may also contribute to insulin resistance—a triple whammy.

STRESS LEADS TO WEIGHT GAIN. A major reason to keep chronic stress in check is that cortisol is known to increase appetite. Yes, that's right: Stress makes you eat more. It also encourages cells in your abdomen to conserve fat—in other words, it packs on the belly weight that seriously raises your risk of a heart attack.

Regularly practicing our relaxation methods will help lower your levels of stress hormones to reverse this trend. It should also help you stick to your eating and exercise goals. Think about it: When you're stressed, you're probably tempted to chow down on whatever fatty, high-calorie snacks are in reach. You're also less likely to stop and think about hitting the pavement for a nice, long walk when you're busy fretting over deadlines, family problems, or that fight with your spouse. When you practice the art of relaxation, you'll step back and see the big picture, and your true priorities—including taking care of your body—will emerge.

Mastering stress has other beneficial "side effects." Specifically, it helps ward off emotional problems that are linked with poor blood sugar control, particularly depression and anger. (Exercise has similar effects, which is another reason it's important to follow Step Five.)

Since stress exists in both your mind and body, our stress-busting techniques tackle it on both fronts. Progress in one automatically creates gains in the other, so if you try two or three of these techniques, you'll reap real results.

1 learn to breathe well

ACTION You probably think breathing comes naturally, but the way we instinctively breathed as babies isn't the way most of us do it as stressed-out adults. The reason: Tension causes the entire body to tighten up, which constricts the lungs and keeps them from filling with air. That makes your breathing shallow and fast. It may sound trivial, but it's not. When your body has trouble getting enough oxygen, it feels even more stressed, which can lead to a faster heartbeat, higher blood pressure, and increased levels of stress hormones that raise blood sugar.

Remarkably, simply breathing more evenly, slowly, and deeply can turn off the body's stress switch and bring blood sugar back down. In fact, there's no better way to instantly exit "full alert" mode. The trick is to make your lungs expand as much as possible, filling them with air from the bottom up. To do that, you'll need to breathe with your belly and stretch your diaphragm muscle, which lies between your chest and abdominal cavity, at the base of your lungs. If you're used to shallow breathing, this may not feel natural at first, and you may even need to strengthen your diaphragm to do it right. The following exercises will develop that muscle and remind your body how to breathe the way nature intended.

SIGH STRATEGICALLY

Ever find yourself sighing and yawning when you're under stress? That's your body's way of getting you to breathe more

A Workout for Your Chest

If you're in the habit of taking short, shallow breaths, your chest and diaphragm muscles are probably out of shape. Get them fit with these tricks.

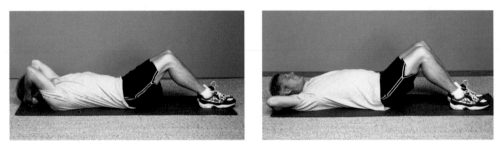

To help your chest expand and boost lung capacity, lie on the floor with your knees bent and your feet flat on the floor. Place your hands behind your head and bring your elbows together so they're nearly touching. As you inhale, slowly let your elbows drop to the sides so your arms are flat on the floor when your lungs are full. As you exhale, raise your elbows again.

Strengthen your diaphragm by giving the muscle some resistance while you're breathing. Wrap a belt around your abdomen, then lie on the floor with your knees bent and your feet flat on the floor. As you exhale, pull on the belt to put pressure on your abdomen. As you inhale, slowly let up on the pressure, but keep the belt tight enough so that your diaphragm must push against it to fill your lungs. An alternative is to press on your abdomen with your hands.

deeply. Kick off your stress-reduction program by building on that sighing instinct. Intentional sighing will help dissolve physical tension and get more oxygen into your system.

1. While sitting or standing straight, with your hands at your sides or resting on your knees, let the air rush out of your lungs as if you were deeply relieved that a stressful event has passed (even if it hasn't).

2. For the moment, forget about how you're breathing in. Just take another breath naturally and let it rush out again.

3. Repeat 10 times for a total of 12 sighs. By the time you've finished, it won't feel like you're sighing anymore. Instead, you'll be breathing deeply.

PRACTICE BELLY BREATHING

Another way to make sure you're breathing properly—and by "properly," we mean from your belly, not your chest—is to practice this deep-breathing exercise. Deep breathing makes tense muscles relax indirectly by signaling to your brain that you've entered a state of rest and peace. Do this exercise daily or anytime you notice that stress is getting the better of you.

1. Find a quiet place and sit comfortably with your back straight against the back of a chair. Place one hand on your chest and the other on your stomach, then breathe normally. Pay attention to which hand moves the most as you inhale and exhale. If it's the one on your chest, the lower areas of your lungs are not filling with air.

2. Take a deep breath through your nose. Inhale slowly so you can't hear your breathing; if the rush of air makes a noise, you're inhaling too quickly. Fill the bottom sections of your lungs first so your diaphragm pushes the hand on your stomach outward. Continue to inhale until you fill the upper parts of your lungs, making the hand on your chest rise slightly.

3. Hold your breath for a moment and think of the word *relax*.

4. Exhale slowly and naturally (it's okay if you can hear the air escaping). Continue breathing in and out slowly for several minutes.

quiz
How to Bust Stress Best

You have lots of options for managing stress. Do you need them all? Knowing more about what bothers you can guide you to techniques that will do the most good. Place a checkmark by any statement that's true of you.

◆ I find it hard to concentrate on the things I need to do.

■ I often find it tough to get going in the morning.

● If another driver cuts ahead of me in traffic, I move up close behind him.

◆ It's common for me to find myself thinking about work problems at home.

● I get very impatient in slow-moving lines at the grocery store or bank.

◆ I often feel tense.

■ I really don't feel I have a lot to look forward to.

● Most people will lie or stab others in the back to get ahead.

◆ My mind is plagued by unsettling thoughts.

● When people are rude or irritating to me, I give them a piece of my mind.

■ When I need to make a decision, it's hard for me to figure out what to do.

◆ I worry quite a lot.

■ I don't feel like talking to people as much as I used to.

◆ It's tough for me to unwind and relax.

● When I feel someone is wrong, there's likely to be an argument.

● People who talk about how hard they have it are just trying to get attention.

◆ I've experienced sexual difficulties recently.

■ I'm so sick of myself, dying would seem like an escape.

◆ I feel insecure much of the time.

● When I'm around someone I dislike, I don't care if I seem rude.

● Most people can't really be trusted.

■ Activities that used to be fun don't seem that way anymore.

● People who tell me what to do usually don't know what they're talking about.

◆ I've been arguing more with my spouse lately.

■ I often feel lonely.

● I've been known to throw things or hit people when I get really angry.

■ There are a lot of days when I can't seem to shake off sad feelings.

■ I feel tired and lethargic a lot of the time.

◆ I find it hard to get a good night's sleep lately.

Continue on the next page.

quiz (continued)

- ● When someone offers me a compliment, I wonder what they want from me.

- ■ It's not unusual for me to break down and cry three or more times a week.

- ◆ I often have aches and pains even if I haven't been exercising.

- ■ My life has been nothing but a series of failures.

- ◆ I'm not sure I can handle everything I need to do.

- ■ I don't really enjoy being around people very much.

- ● Most people would break the law more often if they knew they wouldn't get caught.

What Your Score Means

Count how many of each type of statement you checked.

____ ◆ diamond
____ ■ square
____ ● circle

If you checked four or more ◆ statements, stress is a problem for you. Start by doing deep breathing and correcting irrational thinking, which will produce results fast. When your schedule allows, take time to do progressive muscle relaxation, autogenics, and imagery.

If you checked four or more ■ statements, it's likely that you're depressed. Correcting irrational thinking is likely to benefit you most. If low feelings continue for more than two weeks, however, seek help from a professional therapist.

If you checked four or more ● statements, your biggest problem is anger. You'll benefit most from deep breathing, correcting irrational thinking, and tips for curbing anger.

2 dissolve muscle tension

ACTION Whereas deep breathing works by sending the "stand down" signal, the following exercises work by tackling muscle tension head-on. The first approach we want you to try is progressive muscle relaxation. Studies have found that consistently practicing this technique can lower blood sugar enough to significantly reduce the risk of complications such as kidney disease and eye damage. It can also bring down high blood pressure and help guard against heart disease. And it's simple to learn.

The idea behind progressive muscle relaxation sounds like a contradiction: To make muscles relax, you must first make them tense. The reason it works is that we don't usually notice a lot of the tension in our muscles. Tightening them calls attention to it so you can focus on letting it drain away.

DO A 20-MINUTE **TENSION TAMER**

Twenty minutes is all you need to do a full progressive relaxation routine. To get the most benefit, try to practice this at least once a day, perhaps at bedtime.

Help!

Whenever I'm stressed or upset, I reach for food.

Welcome to the emotional eater club. It's no surprise that food is tied to feelings. As kids, our parents nurtured and rewarded us with food. As adults, we equate food with socializing, relaxing, and having fun. As a result, it can be comforting when you're feeling low or edgy and stimulating when you're feeling bored.

- First, make sure you're not genuinely hungry. If it's been more than 4 or 5 hours since you last ate, have a low-fat snack, such as a piece of fruit. Note what you feel like eating: If any food would satisfy you, you're probably truly hungry. If you crave a specific food, your "hunger" is probably driven by emotions.
- Wait it out. Cravings often vanish as fast as they appear. Instead of eating, play with your dog, call a friend, or finish a small chore.
- Get out of the house, or at least the kitchen. In other words, take yourself out of the way of temptation.
- Take a detour after work to defuse stress so you're not so tempted by the bounty of your fridge and pantry when you get home. A stroll through the park should do the trick.
- Find other ways to indulge. Food isn't the only way to treat yourself. If you can raise your spirits by shopping, reading a trashy novel, or getting a massage, go for broke.

1. While either lying down or sitting in a comfortable chair that supports your head, close your eyes and start by mentally scanning your body for places that feel tense.

2. Follow the serenity sequence on the opposite page, clenching each muscle area as tightly as you can and holding for 5 seconds. Take about 20 seconds to gradually release the tension, consciously relaxing your muscles as much as possible, then move on to the next area.

3. Silently repeat a soothing thought, such as "I am totally calm" or "Goodbye, tension."

RELAX TO A EURYTHMIC BEAT

No, we're not talking about the British rock band from the '80s. Eurythmics is a music education technique developed by a Swiss composer who believed the body is finely tuned to musical rhythms. Some relaxation therapists have adopted his methods to combine full-body muscle relaxation with deep breathing in a meditative rhythm set to the tick-tock of a metronome. Here's how to do it.

- Set a metronome so it ticks off one beat per second (or use a ticking clock).

- Inhale for a count of six, hold your breath for one count, then exhale for a count of six. (You can take more than six beats to inhale and exhale if your lungs take longer than that to fill.)

- Repeat the breathing exercise, but this time, gradually tense all your muscles for the count of six. Hold the tension for one count, relax your body for a count of six, and pause for a count of one.

- Continue tensing and relaxing your entire body in time with your breathing, or use each cycle of counting to focus on isolated areas, such as your arms, legs, torso, and head.

ARM YOURSELF WITH AUTOGENICS

Like progressive muscle relaxation, autogenics—a form of self-hypnosis—harnesses the power of the imagination to make the body relax. Therapists sometimes use it in

Hands: Clench your fists, then relax.

Arms: Bend your dominant arm at the elbow and tense your biceps and lower arm as hard as you can without clenching your fist. Relax and repeat with the other arm.

Forehead: Raise your eyebrows and wrinkle your forehead as tightly as you can, then relax while picturing your forehead becoming smooth. Next, deeply furrow your brow into a frown and relax.

Lips: Press your lips and front teeth together, then relax.

Neck: Press your head into the back of your chair, then relax. Bend your neck and move your chin down onto your chest. As you relax, let your head return to a comfortable upright position.

Shoulders: Shrug your shoulders up toward your ears as far as is comfortable. As you release, note the relaxation you feel in your neck.

Abdomen: Pull your navel in toward your backbone, then relax.

Buttocks: Squeeze your buttocks together, then relax.

Thighs: Push your heels against the floor, then relax.

Calves and feet: Curl your toes toward the floor, keeping your heels flat, then relax.

Shins: Raise your toes off the floor, then relax.

Eyes: Squeeze your eyes shut as tightly as you can, then relax, keeping your eyelids closed.

Jaw: Tighten your jaw so your back teeth clench together. Gradually relax, ending with your lips slightly parted.

conjunction with biofeedback, but you don't need to be hooked to a machine that monitors your body functions to benefit from it. All you need is a quiet room and a comfortable chair that supports your head, back, and arms. Or you can sit slightly stooped on a stool, with your arms resting on your thighs and your hands hanging loosely between your knees.

After you're settled into position with your eyes closed, do the following sequence.

1. Concentrate your attention on your dominant arm, usually the right. Slowly repeat "My right arm is heavy" in your mind and imagine the arm actually becoming heavier. Pause after the statement, repeating it four times.

2. Do the same with your left arm.

3. Next, repeat the exercise using the words "Both my arms are heavy."

4. Concentrate on your right leg and slowly repeat "My right leg is heavy" four times.

5. Do the same with your left leg, then both legs.

6. Repeat the exercise, but this time use the word *warm* instead of *heavy* and imagine your limbs becoming warmer.

Once you're used to this technique, you can do another exercise in which you imagine your limbs becoming heavier and warmer at the same time. It's possible that you'll enter a trance-like state—which is fine. When you're finished with the exercise, simply mark its completion by telling yourself, "When I open my eyes, I will be refreshed and alert."

SCHEDULE A **MASSAGE**

Who could imagine that something as luxuriously indulgent as a massage could actually help you manage diabetes? But it can. Anecdotal evidence suggests that a massage can temporarily lower blood sugar significantly. Nothing is more relaxing than a massage, and, as you've already learned, relaxation lowers levels of stress hormones, which in turn lowers blood sugar. Massage also boosts blood circulation, which is often less than ideal in people with diabetes. In short, massage isn't just about being pampered; it's also about your health.

Of course, a massage from a professional massage therapist is best. Check local spas and gyms to find massage services, or ask your doctor for a referral. Swedish massage, the most common type, is the one generally used for relaxation. Because your blood sugar could drop during the massage, tell the therapist that you have diabetes, and be prepared with a sugary snack. If you take insulin, be aware that massage may increase your body's uptake of the insulin at the injection site and send your blood sugar down in a hurry.

If you can't or don't want to spend the money for a professional massage, ask a friend or relative to give you a massage using light, unscented lotion or massage oil. You can also give yourself a soothing mini-massage. In one small study at New Mexico State University, type 2 diabetes patients' blood sugar fell after six weekly stress-busting sessions that included gripping the fingers, squeezing the arms, and pressing the head— all body areas that you can easily reach to do self-massages such as these.

- Grasp and twist your right forefinger between the thumb and fingers of your left hand, sliding from the base to the tip of the finger as you twist. Repeat twice with each finger of your right hand, then repeat on your left hand.

- Take hold of your right forearm so that your left thumb is positioned just below your right palm. Use your thumb to stroke up the forearm to the elbow. Turn your arm over and massage the top of the forearm as well, then repeat on the other arm.

- Place four fingertips of each hand on top of your head and press down, moving your fingertips in a circular motion.

3 picture serenity now

ACTION Tranquil thoughts are like water bubbling from a spring that percolates into a flowing stream and nourishes the world around it. Stressful thoughts, on the other hand, are like an overwhelming flood. Control the water, and you keep havoc under control so that everything remains calm, serene, and marked by the pure, quiet sound of gurgling.

In case you didn't notice, all that talk about tranquil, flowing water makes use of imagery, a powerful technique for focusing thoughts on peaceful mental pictures and triggering the feelings that go with them. Think it's corny? Don't knock it. It's clear that even subtle thoughts and feelings can have an impact on blood sugar. For example, lab mice bred to have diabetes have higher blood sugar when they are conditioned to merely *anticipate* a minor annoyance such as the floor under their feet moving.

The following exercises use a variety of meditative techniques that harness some form of imagery. To do them, find a quiet place where you can sit undisturbed for up to 20 minutes. Use the deep-breathing techniques you've already learned while you take your mind through the exercises. To make the images easier to conjure up, consider recording the instructions on an audiotape so you don't have to memorize or refer to them.

Don't worry if you find unwanted thoughts intruding while you're using imagery: When thoughts shoved to the recesses of your mind start moving into your consciousness, it's actually a sign that you're letting go of the stress that was holding them back. Just passively let them move through your mind, then turn back to the exercise.

COLOR YOUR WORLD

There's no need to conjure up detailed scenes to begin with. Many people find that even picturing simple colors can promote feelings of peace and calm.

1. Close your eyes and imagine your entire field of vision filled with a single color. It doesn't matter which color you choose; try different ones and settle on whatever color is easiest to hold in your mind.

2. Imagine the color becoming punctuated with areas of lighter and darker shades. Picture the shades drifting slowly about like clouds in the sky.

3. Next, imagine another color appearing in a simple geometric shape, such as a circle or triangle. Focus on this new color while you take several deep breaths, then imagine that another color appears in a different shape.

4. Have the shapes begin moving slowly around in your mind's eye and give them different dimensions, so a square

becomes a cube or a triangle becomes a cone. Let them slowly tumble and move through space. Add other shapes if you wish, or change the color of the background.

TAKE A MENTAL GETAWAY

Now it's time to really let your imagination loose. Even though you can't escape to a beautiful, peaceful place whenever stress rears its ugly head, if you can imagine such a place—including all the sights, sounds, smells, and even the temperature—you can experience it. The scenario you choose is up to you. Here's one example.

1. Picture yourself on a mountaintop surrounded by lush trop-ical vegetation but open to the sky, so you're bathed in sunlight. Note the deep blue color of the sky, feel the sun's rays soothing your body, smell the fragrance of the flowers all around, and hear the patter of drops falling off leaves after a recent rain. Look far below and see the shore of a tranquil beach on a placid lake.

2. Take yourself to the shore of the lake and imagine walking along the soft sand. You're completely alone, but you find a boat tied to a dock. After untying the mooring rope, lie down on soft blankets inside the boat and watch the clouds as you drift on the calm water. The boat rocks gently, and waves gurgle under the hull as you drink in the warmth and feel the soft movement of a breeze. You feel a deep sense of relaxation as you drift between the water and the clouds.

TRY THE "PINK BUBBLE" TECHNIQUE

Build on your powers of imagination to create more sophisti-cated images that are tied to your goals or desires. Use this amazingly simple but potentially powerful technique when everyday stresses—a crotchety boss, an illness, family diffi-culties—seem to prevent you from realizing your dreams, which can create a sense of powerlessness and frustration.

1. Sit quietly with your eyes closed and imagine that a dream or goal has already been fulfilled—perhaps you have a new job, you're on your ideal vacation, or you're retired and living someplace warm and beautiful.

2. Imagine the scene becoming surrounded by a translucent pink bubble, a color associated with the heart. Watch as the scene enclosed in the pink bubble begins to lift and slowly float away. Breathe deeply as you imagine the scene floating through the universe, gathering energy for a time when it will return to you. Let go of frustration as you wait for the day the scene comes back.

ACTION 4 use real-life anti-stress strategies

Fights with spouses, health problems, money woes—things happen. To everyone, not just you. When they do, how do you react? Do you panic and imagine that divorce, death, or financial ruin is imminent? You see, it's not necessarily the things life throws at you that cause stress (and raise blood sugar), but rather your reaction to them.

Two common types of thinking can easily act against you. One is assuming the worst—for example, automatically believing that because your boss is in a bad mood, you're going to be fired. The other is believing that you, other people, the world, and life in general have to live up to certain standards—which leads to disappointment and frustration when they inevitably don't. Stress-inducing thoughts often revolve around irrational beliefs such as:

- It's necessary that everyone like me.
- If people disapprove of me, I must be wrong or bad.
- I have to be competent in everything I do.
- My value as a person depends on what I achieve.
- It's terrible when things aren't the way I want.
- People are the victims of their circumstances.
- I'm entitled to a good life and should never experience pain.

When you identify underlying beliefs like these, you'll find it easier to counter this negative thinking that can add to stress and bring you down.

STOP NEGATIVE THOUGHTS

To stop negative reactions in their tracks, try the following strategies.

1. Start by writing down (or thinking clearly about) exactly what happened in an upsetting situation. Take a just-the-facts approach and skip any value judgments or conjectures. Some examples of facts: Your boss seemed irritated this morning. Your child disobeyed you. Your spouse worked late.

2. Note what you're telling yourself about this supposedly terrible event and how it makes you feel. Include all your assumptions, predictions, and beliefs. If your boss is irritated, these might include "I must have done something wrong"; "He's always in a bad mood when I'm around, so he must hate me"; or "He acted like this the last time he let someone go, so he's probably going to again."

3. Challenge your assumptions. Is your boss's irritation really about you, or could there be another cause? Is he really this way all the time? Hasn't he been angry many times without firing anybody?

4. Change what you tell yourself to fit the evidence. For example, "My boss is irritated, but he's always that way. It probably has nothing to do with me" or "I can't be responsible for my boss's mood—only my own."

A Guide to "Get Real" Thinking

Whenever you feel stressed by the way someone treats you or the turn your life is taking, keep the following touchstones in mind.

> **Stress is about me, not the situation.** An airplane flight may panic someone who's never flown but seem mind-numbingly dull to a business traveler. The right perspective will enable you to handle any situation.
> **What's done is done.** Lots of things happen for reasons that are beyond your control, and thinking "would have," "could have," or "should have" won't help you deal with an existing situation. Instead, think in future-oriented terms, such as "I hope" or "next time."
> **Nobody's perfect—including me.** Expect a reasonable amount of failure and disappointment from both yourself and others, then adopt an attitude of forgiveness.

PUT A **STOP SIGN** IN YOUR BRAIN

In research at Duke University, one of the techniques that proved helpful for people with diabetes was a simple method known as thought stopping. Use it any time negative or irrational thinking starts to get the better of you.

1. Close your eyes and imagine a situation in which the stressful thought might spring into your head. Set a

timer for 3 minutes and continue contemplating the stressful thought.

2. When the timer goes off, shout "Stop!" You may want to punctuate your exclamation with a physical sign, such as standing up or clapping your hands. (This may seem awkward at first, but the forcefulness of the statement is part of what makes it work. As you become more experienced with the technique, you can say the word more quietly or think it to yourself.) Try to keep your mind blank for 30 seconds, and if the thought comes back, shout "Stop" again.

3. Replace the distressing thought with another thought that's more positive and rational. For example, if the stressful thought is "I can't do this; I'm worthless," instead say to yourself, "There are many valuable things I can do."

HANDLE HOSTILITY

Do you always feel at war with the people around you? Do you lean on the horn if the person in front of you is driving too slowly? Is your first response to a difficult situation to get angry? If so, you may have the type of personality that's been shown to raise blood sugar.

Researchers have long suspected that anger and hostility play a role in heart disease. More recent findings suggest that people who are typically angry or show related traits such as cynicism, rage, and aggression also tend to have higher blood sugar and insulin resistance. Another problem: Angry or hostile people are more likely to overeat. One study, for example, found that people who tended to be hostile ate 600 more calories a day than people who were less angry.

You can't change your personality, but it's entirely possible to dial down angry thinking and behavior. Techniques such as deep breathing and the tricks you just learned are the best place to start. In fact, programs using stress management and relaxation training to manage anger have been shown to lower rates of heart attack, and Duke researchers believe the same approaches can help control blood sugar.

Beyond those techniques, you can take a number of practical steps to keep momentary flare-ups from becoming infernos.

GET AWAY. Sometimes the only way to keep from blowing your top is to leave the situation that's provoking you until you can calm down. Best bet: Take an exercise break. If it's not

Negative Thoughts Workshop

Catching yourself in the act of negative thinking is the first step in stopping it. When you notice you have a negative thought, write it down in the left column. Then find a way to "spin" the thought into a more positive one. (We've given you a few examples to get you started.) To get more mileage out of this exercise, speak the positive thoughts into a tape recorder and play the messages back to yourself.

NEGATIVE THOUGHT	POSITIVE THOUGHT
I'm disorganized and can't get everything done.	If I take more time for myself, I'll have more energy and focus.
I'll never reach my weight-loss goal.	If I can lose just a little bit of weight, that's a good start.

possible to physically get away from the situation, distract your mind by counting to 10; that's timeless advice because it works.

BE SPECIFIC. When confronting someone you're angry with, don't launch into a laundry list of perceived faults and slights. Instead, focus on the one thing that's really bothering you—and be sure to figure out what that is before you speak up. Say exactly what you would like to see changed to make the situation better.

AVOID INSULTS. It may be tempting to "explain" how another person is being inconsiderate or boorish, but you won't make headway in solving the real issue (getting more help from a spouse, how much money to spend on vacation) if the other person is too busy being defensive to listen.

You will also help yourself by seeking out the company of positive people and limiting your exposure to negative or irritating people.

ACTION 5 lower blood sugar with sleep

A really basic way to feel less stressed during the day—and one that most of us fail to capitalize on—is to get enough sleep at night.

Wouldn't it be great if you could go to bed and wake up with better blood sugar control? In effect, that may be what you do when you get adequate sleep. Recent research suggests that not getting the shuteye you need may contribute to insulin resistance. One reason is that poor sleepers often experience sleep apnea, a condition that interferes with normal breathing and has been linked to diabetes. But there's also evidence that sleep by itself helps the body use glucose more efficiently.

One study found that people who got only about 5 hours of sleep had 40 percent lower insulin sensitivity than people who got about 8 hours. Are you getting enough sleep? Probably not: Most people get at least 60 to 90 minutes less than they need.

If this sounds like a problem with a simple (and enjoyable) solution, it is: Spend more time in the sack. But getting enough sleep is as much about quality as quantity, and it's not always easy to drift off when you want to, especially when you're under stress. Fortunately, if you've followed the 10 Percent Plan up to this point, you're already doing plenty that will help you get good sleep: eating right, exercising, and managing stress. If you still need help, however, try these tips.

DON'T SLEEP IN. Snoozing late on weekends seems an obvious way to catch up on your winks, but it may be doing more harm than good by throwing your body out of rhythm, which can make it more difficult to get to sleep at night. If you're going to add sleep time, do it by going to bed earlier and getting up at the usual time. Then try to stick to your new schedule so that your body clock knows when to cue feelings of sleepiness at night.

RESERVE YOUR BEDROOM FOR SLEEP. Keep the TV out of the bedroom, and don't pay bills or do other paperwork in bed.

DIAL DOWN YOUR MENTAL ENERGY AT NIGHT. Put down that page-turner well ahead of bedtime, and if at all possible, don't start conversations that could lead to disagreements.

LEAVE YOUR WORRIES ON PAPER. If you find yourself bombarded by worries at night, take a half hour before bed to record your concerns and jot down possible solutions. When you feel you've dealt with an issue, you're more likely to drift off.

KNOW WHEN TO FOLD. If you can't sleep after 30 minutes, get out of bed, or you'll just get frustrated with your efforts to fall asleep. (In one study, volunteers who were offered $25 to fall asleep quickly took longer to nod off than those who weren't under any pressure.) Keep the lights low and pick up a boring book or tune into dull TV program until you feel sleepy again.

IF YOU WAKE UP DURING THE NIGHT, STAY IN BED. You'll have a better chance of falling back to sleep, and your body will be getting rest, even if you're not sleeping.

etes

(di•a•be•tes), *noun*

1. A metabolic disorder usually char-
acterized by inadequate secretion
or utilization of insulin and exces-
sive amounts of glucose in the
blood and urine.

2. A disease causing high blood
sugar, which can be lowered using
massage, herbs, and other alternative approaches, as well as with
lifestyle changes and medications.

PART THREE

Beyond the 10 Percent Plan

other
natural
approaches

Well-timed eating, balanced meals, healthy portion sizes, exercise, stress relief—these are the essential natural solutions to diabetes contained in the 10 Percent Plan. Are there other measures beyond these that can help keep blood sugar under control? Yes.

In this chapter, you'll read about the most promising alternative approaches to managing diabetes and its complications.

These approaches, from acupuncture and herbs to minerals and magnet therapy, aren't officially part of the plan because their effects are less well studied than those of diet and exercise. Certainly, none of them can *replace* diet and exercise if you want to lose weight and permanently improve your health, but some of them may help. Weigh the evidence for yourself and decide, with your doctor, whether you want to try them.

Modern medicine has given us an array of weapons to fight diabetes, many of which weren't available even a decade ago. Take the best-selling drug metformin (Glucophage). It dams the release of glucose from the liver, slows the absorption of glucose from food, lowers blood levels of triglycerides (which helps fight heart disease), and may even help people with diabetes lose weight. But don't give chemists and synthetic compounds all the credit: Metformin is derived from French lilac, a traditional remedy for high blood sugar.

So-called alternative treatments such as herbs and supplements can't hold a candle to the power of conventional drugs—at least they haven't in studies so far. Nevertheless, there's no doubt that some of them may be able to influence blood sugar. Should you try an alternative approach? Chances are, you've already done so. In a recent survey published in the *American Journal of Public Health*, 57 percent of people with diabetes said they had tried complementary and alternative medicine within the previous year, and 34 percent said they had tried treatments specifically for diabetes. But here's an interesting twist: Some of the therapies that may be most promising are relatively little used. Fewer than 7 percent of people with diabetes surveyed take herbs that studies suggest may help control blood sugar.

There are plenty of reasons to be wary of herbs and supplements you find on supermarket and drugstore shelves and in health food stores. First, the supplement industry is not regulated (except in the rare cases where a product appears to be blatantly dangerous), so you can't be sure you're getting a product that works, or even that you're getting the herb or nutrient advertised on the label (and there's no guarantee it will work if you do). Why not? Natural medicines can't be patented, so there's not much incentive for companies to shell out big money to prove their effectiveness.

Still, there are glimmers of potential in the small amount of research that does exist. The therapies you'll find on the following pages are those that show the most promise for helping to control diabetes or some of its major complications. Because

Involving Your Doctor

There was a time when doctors were openly hostile to alternative approaches to medicine. That's changing, because doctors have seen for themselves that natural approaches sometimes work and because they want patients who use these treatments to keep them in the loop. If you decide to try one of the therapies in this chapter, talk to your doctor before starting. He may even be able to refer you to a local practitioner, such as an herbalist or acupuncturist. Be sure to keep him informed once you start your therapy.

they've undergone relatively little research, regimens and doses can only be suggested and shouldn't be taken as medical recommendations. In fact, it's worth repeating that we don't actually *recommend* any of these treatments. If you choose to look into them on your own, here's information that may help guide your choices.

Assessing Acupuncture

Can you really bring down blood sugar by having your skin poked with thin needles? Practitioners of traditional Chinese medicine (TCM) say yes—but for reasons well outside the realm of Western medicine. According to the philosophy of TCM, diseases come from imbalances in the flow of life energy, which courses through the body along invisible pathways called meridians. Acupuncture, which involves inserting needles at specific points in the meridian system, is said to bring this energy into balance and improve health. Different points are associated with specific physical functions. Stimulating the pancreas "acupoint," for example, may increase insulin secretion, while probing the bladder acupoint may help with frequent urination.

Western doctors used to dismiss acupuncture wholesale. It just didn't make sense, especially when the meridian system didn't appear to be related to any obvious part of the anatomy. Nowadays, however, some insurance plans cover acupuncture for certain conditions related to diabetes, and it's not unusual to find medical doctors who are also trained acupuncturists.

The change is due in part to rigorous studies in the West that have found that acupuncture can be effective for relieving pain, making it especially promising for people who have neuropathy. In one recent study, for example, 77 percent of people with neuropathic pain improved significantly after receiving acupuncture—and 67 percent were able to stop taking pain medication. Some said their symptoms cleared up completely, and most never had to go back for more treatment. How does acupuncture achieve such results? It's been shown that acupoints have denser-than-usual concentrations of nerves, and stimulating them appears to make the brain release natural painkillers.

Whether acupuncture can lower blood sugar is less certain. Most of the research showing an effect has been done in

China, where studies don't always live up to Western scientific standards. But one review of several Chinese studies, published in the *Journal of Traditional Chinese Medicine*, found that acupuncture consistently lowered blood sugar in people with diabetes by about 50 percent. In one of the more dramatic of these studies, average blood sugar dropped from 21 to 6.5 after acupuncture treatments.

IF YOU TRY IT: Don't expect dramatic blood sugar results. Medical societies, such as the World Health Organization, recommend acupuncture for a wide variety of problems, but type 2 diabetes doesn't appear on their hit lists. Neuropathy does, however. Just be sure to tell your practitioner if you have neuropathy or poor circulation: The therapist will want to be extra cautious when needling the slow-healing skin of your lower legs and feet.

Typically, you'll feel a prick, a tingling sensation, or a dull ache when needles first go in, but the feeling quickly goes away. Treatment usually involves inserting needles in 4 to 12 acupoints and leaving them there for 15 to 30 minutes. Once the needles are in place, practitioners often twist or manipulate them by hand to regulate the flow of energy in the body, which produces a dull ache that can be uncomfortable but is thought to be important for releasing chemicals into the nervous system. Needles may also be heated or charged with low-level electrical current.

You can expect to pay anywhere from $50 to $150 per treatment, which can add up: In studies, therapy for diabetes typically takes multiple sessions. To find a listing of practitioners, try the Canadian Society of Chinese Medicine and Acupuncture website at www.tcmcanada.org/english/practitioners.html.

Investigating Herbal Alternatives

Some of the most promising alternative treatments for high blood sugar come from nature's pharmacy, which isn't surprising. Plants and herbs have long been part of traditional treatment for diabetes, and they may be the closest thing to "real" medicine in the entire alternative arsenal. In fact, some countries, such as Germany, require doctors to study herbal medicine as part of their medical training. That's why it's important to respect the potential power of herbs and use them with a measure of caution.

Be sure to check with your doctor before using any herbal remedy, even if you're taking it for something other than diabetes. Many herbs can affect blood pressure and liver function, and they may interfere with medications you're already taking. If you're taking an herbal supplement, it's critical to closely monitor your blood sugar to guard against hypoglycemia; help your doctor decide how to make any adjustments in your drug treatment; and, of course, to tell if it's working. If it is, keep in mind that it shouldn't take the place of medication or insulin, even if it allows you to use those treatments in lower doses.

GYMNEMA: THE SUGAR BLASTER

In India and Africa, where *Gymnema sylvestre* can be found creeping in tropical forests, this woody plant has been used for centuries as a remedy for diabetes. In fact, its name in Hindi is *gurmar*, which means "sugar destroyer." It got its reputation in part because chewing its leaves is said to make you insensible to the taste of sweetness, but there's probably more to it than that. Lab analyses have found that gymnema boosts the activity of enzymes that help cells take up glucose, so there's less of it floating in the blood. More than a decade ago, animal studies found that it brings down blood sugar—but not in animals that had had their pancreases removed. These revelations have led researchers to theorize that gymnema may battle high blood sugar by:

- Boosting the release of insulin by making cells in the pancreas more permeable
- Stimulating insulin-making beta cells in the pancreas
- Increasing the number of beta cells

Does it work in people? Herbalists believe that if any herb is going to bring down your blood sugar, it's gymnema, but there haven't been a lot of good studies to back up that assertion. Still, the research that's been done has been tantalizing. In one study from a medical institute in India, for example, type 2 diabetes patients who took gymnema in addition to medication reduced their average blood sugar levels more than a control group that took only the drug. About a quarter of those taking gymnema were able to stop using the medication altogether. Similar results have been seen in research on people with type 1 diabetes.

IF YOU TRY IT: Expect an effect—and be sure to tell your doctor so he can coordinate your herb doses with the rest of your treatment. Safety studies haven't been done on gymnema, but it has a long history and no known reports of nasty side effects. The lack of data makes gymnema inappropriate for women who are pregnant or nursing, but beyond that, the main concern is that blood sugar may fall too low, especially if the herb is taken with a diabetes medication. Typical doses are 400 to 600 mg a day.

FENUGREEK:
A POTENT SPICE

In Mediterranean and Near Eastern countries, fenugreek has a long history as a spice and flavor enhancer, but that's not all it's been used for over the centuries. Early Greek and Latin catalogs of medicines list it as a treatment for high blood sugar. Animal research and a handful of small human studies suggest the ancients were on to something. In one study, for example, 60 people with type 2 diabetes who took a total of 25 g of fenugreek powder in two equal doses at lunch and dinner for six months dropped their fasting blood sugar from an average of 8.4 to 6.2.

Fenugreek seems to make the stomach empty more slowly, hinder the absorption of carbohydrates, and put the brakes on the movement of glucose through the body—all of which may be due to the fact that fenugreek is extremely high in fiber. Given its family history, that's not surprising: Fenugreek is a legume, like lentils, chickpeas, and peanuts.

How Good Is the Proof?

Can thousands of satisfied users of an alternative therapy be wrong? In the eyes of science, yes. Proof (or at least convincing evidence) lies in carefully conducted studies; everything else is just a step above hearsay. Why are researchers such sticklers? Here's what they look for.

▸ **Studies in which people in one group get the real treatment and people in a control group get a dummy treatment (placebo).** Without a control group, some people may feel better (or say they do) simply because they expect to—or because improvements are really due to something other than the treatment.

▸ **Studies in which neither the participants nor the researchers know who is getting the real thing and who is getting the placebo.** That's another way to make sure positive results are due to the treatment and not to expectations from subjects who have been tipped off, perhaps by researchers themselves.

▸ **Studies that involve large numbers of people** to make sure the results aren't a fluke, are published in respected journals, and are reviewed by experts to make sure the research is up to snuff.

IF YOU TRY IT: Fenugreek rides a fine line between being a supplement or a food. In one study, volunteers took their daily doses by eating defatted fenugreek seed powder, which has a mild, nutty taste, in unleavened bread. You can also make tea by soaking the seeds in cold water. Adding fenugreek to your diet is the ideal way to get it, because taking therapeutic doses in capsules can mean downing a lot of pills. (One tablespoon of powder weighs just over 10 g, and some studies have called for as much as 50 g twice a day.) One way to consume it: Mix 25 to 50 g of fenugreek seed powder with vegetables or fruit in a blender to make a smoothie.

Although it can cause flatulence and diarrhea, fenugreek is generally considered safe; in a few rare instances, people have had severe reactions to it. As with most remedies that haven't been well tested, you should avoid fenugreek if you're pregnant or nursing or have liver or kidney disease. And don't take it within 2 hours of taking a diabetes medication, as it may interfere with your body's absorption of the drug.

BITTER MELON: A STRONG VEGETABLE

Although it's a staple of Chinese and Indian cuisine, bitter melon lives up to its name—or names: It's also known as bitter gourd, bitter apple, and bitter cucumber. Cultivated in tropical areas of Asia, Africa, and South America, it's been used as a contraceptive, a treatment for psoriasis, and a variety of other purposes. Mainly, though, it's been hailed for lowering blood sugar, and the fruit and seeds are loaded with chemicals that appear to have an impact on glucose or insulin (one of the chemicals is similar to cow insulin).

Lab and animal studies suggest that bitter melon may work on several levels, such as boosting insulin secretion, improving the ability of cells to absorb glucose, and hindering the release of glucose from the liver. One of the largest studies of bitter melon in people with type 2 diabetes lasted only two days, but

Another Reason to Try Ginseng

Ginseng has a reputation as a cure-all—but if it's supposed to affect *everything*, can it really be that good at *anything*? In the case of diabetes, at least one carefully controlled study published in a respected medical journal recently found that taking 3 g of American ginseng *(Panax quinquefolius)*, commercially grown in Canada and exported to China, brought blood sugar down by 20 percent as measured by a standard glucose test. Animal studies suggest that ginseng may lower blood sugar by slowing absorption of carbohydrates or boosting cells' uptake of glucose.

it caused significant drops in blood sugar for 100 participants within hours of drinking suspended vegetable pulp. A number of smaller but longer trials have had similar results.

IF YOU TRY IT: You can get bitter melon at health food stores or Asian grocery stores in a variety of forms, including powder, extract, juice, and the raw vegetable. Herbalists often suggest taking it in juice (50 ml [2 oz]—is a typical daily dose), but if you don't like the bitter taste, you may want to consider capsules instead; 3 to 15 g daily is usually recommended. Look for products that are made from the fruit or seeds—the apparent source of bitter melon's effects—not the leaves or vine.

Bitter melon is widely used in Asia and appears to be safe for most adults, but it's thought to interfere with fertility, so you shouldn't take it if you're pregnant or hoping to become pregnant. Keep it out of the reach of children: A number of reports suggest it's toxic to young bodies, and at least one child is known to have died from drinking the juice.

Nutrient Micromanagement

All those vegetables you're eating on the 10 Percent Plan will probably mean you're getting more nutrients than just about anybody else you know. Despite that, some micronutrients may be worth taking in supplement form when you have type 2 diabetes.

Micronutrients are substances that the body needs in only very small amounts but have powerful (though often subtle) effects. Many are involved with metabolism, and being even moderately deficient in them may contribute to chronic diseases. Getting more of certain micronutrients appears to help control diabetes. People with diabetes may be low in some of these because frequent urination may flush them from the body quickly.

Do you need more micronutrients? Because they're poorly understood, it's difficult to say for sure. That's one reason it makes sense to take a daily multivitamin that ensures you get at least the minimal amounts researchers believe you need to keep your body healthy. Beyond that, supplemental doses of specific micronutrients that aren't found in most multivitamins may help keep your glucose under better control.

CONTROL WITH **CHROMIUM**

Although it sounds like something you'd use to polish your wheel covers, chromium is actually a trace mineral that helps the body use glucose. For example, chromium appears to make it easier for insulin to bind with cells so that glucose can enter tissues and not build up in the blood. Despite its importance, most Canadians probably don't get enough each day because it is found in only trace amounts in food. It's estimated that we should get 50 to 200 mcg (micrograms).

Will getting more give you a hand with blood sugar control? Even though chromium is one of the better known micronutrients suggested for diabetes, research with people who have high blood sugar has produced mixed results. In one of the largest studies, 180 people were assigned to groups that got either chromium (two different doses were tried) or a dummy pill. Those who got the chromium significantly reduced their A1C numbers (which indicate long-term blood sugar control) after four months, and those who got the highest dose (1,000 mcg) lowered their cholesterol as well. Several other studies have shown similar results, but in some others, chromium either had no effect on blood sugar or the findings were ambiguous.

Garlic for the Heart

Diabetes is linked to heart disease, which has its own arsenal of herbal medicines. Leading them is garlic, which has been shown to reduce "bad" LDL cholesterol by about 16 percent and lower blood pressure. In one study, garlic actually trimmed plaque by about 3 percent in the arteries of people who took it. And there's a bonus: Some studies find garlic lowers blood sugar as well. Just be sure you don't take garlic if you're taking a blood thinner (it will thin blood even more), and don't cook it if you want medicinal benefits, because heat changes its chemistry. The best way to tap garlic's powers: Eat it raw—then stay home for the night.

You may have heard that chromium helps the body lose fat without shaving muscle, and some research points in that direction. In one study of 122 moderately overweight people, those who took 400 mcg of chromium a day saw an average weight loss of 2.8 kg (6.2 lb) over the course of three months. Few other studies have backed these findings, and you'll probably be disappointed if you take chromium for weight loss.

IF YOU TRY IT: The biggest blood sugar benefits have been seen in people who eat a low-chromium diet, which typically includes a lot of sugar and refined white flour—low-chromium foods that actually trigger chromium loss. Since you're already avoiding those foods on the 10 Percent Plan, you're ahead of the game from the start.

If you take a supplement, stick to the recommended daily amount of 200 mcg or less: Chromium is a heavy metal, and large doses may build up in the body, potentially leading to kidney damage. Chromium comes in different forms, but most studies use chromium picolinate, which the body absorbs better than another type, chromium chloride.

BOOST INSULIN SENSITIVITY WITH **VANADIUM**

When a Swedish chemist discovered this trace element, he named it after Vanadis, the Scandinavian goddess of youth and beauty, because of its lovely colors. In the 19th century, before the discovery of insulin, a form of vanadium was used to treat diabetes, and it now appears that it influences insulin's performance in a variety of ways. In animals, it's been shown to help cells take up glucose; in lab studies with rats, high doses of vanadium (thousands of times greater than the amount thought necessary for good health) have brought down elevated blood sugar.

Small human studies using more reasonable doses have shown promising effects as well. For example, research at Harvard's Joslin Diabetes Center found that vanadium improves insulin sensitivity in people with type 2 diabetes and lowers cholesterol as well. Does it bring down blood sugar numbers? That's what happened in a study at Temple University in Philadelphia in which people with type 2 diabetes took 50 mcg of vanadyl sulfate, one form of vanadium, for three weeks.

IF YOU TRY IT: Because you need only tiny amounts of vanadium (daily needs are estimated at a minuscule 10 to 30 mcg), it doesn't take much extra to hit toxic levels. Although nobody knows the body's upper tolerances, research suggests you should limit doses to no more than 100 mcg a day. (You probably already get about 20 mcg from your diet.)

Look for products containing vanadyl sulfate, which is thought to be less toxic than sodium metavandate, the other major form of vanadium. Lower the dose if you experience nausea, vomiting, cramping, or diarrhea—all common side effects. And be sure to let your doctor know if you're taking vanadium, especially if you're on a blood-thinning medication, since vanadium may interfere with it.

Help for Nerve Damage

No supplement or therapy is going to cure you of neuropathy, but if you have the irritation, pain, and tingling of this common diabetes complication, even a little bit of relief can make a big difference. Because nerve damage can affect so many aspects of your health (including your sense of touch and pain, sexual function, and digestion), the first order of business is to keep high blood sugar from causing more harm. If you're doing everything you can with diet, exercise, and medical treatment, it may be time to look into other options.

THE ALLURE OF **Alpha-Lipoic Acid**

What causes diabetic neuropathy? One theory is that neuropathy begins when nerve cells swell. If you trace reasons for the swelling back several steps, it appears that glucose teams up with an enzyme to draw water into cells and not let it out. That's where alpha-lipoic acid, or ALA, comes in. This powerful antioxidant is thought to block the troublesome enzyme that leads to swelling. What's more, ALA protects cells against the damaging effects of free radicals, destructive molecules that are also thought to play a role in nerve damage.

The body makes small amounts of ALA, and you get a bit more from foods such as spinach, but these sources don't provide enough to do battle against neuropathy. For that, you need a supplement. Can ALA help people with nerve damage feel better? Belief that it can is strong, and researchers have looked into ALA more rigorously than they have most other alternative therapies.

While results are still not conclusive, they have been encouraging. In one trial involving 328 people with type 2 diabetes, those who received ALA injections every day for three weeks felt significantly less pain from neuropathy than those who didn't get the treatment. An even larger follow-up trial, however, failed to find much of an effect from ALA.

To get a handle on the balance of evidence, researchers at a German diabetes institute recently reviewed four different well-controlled studies and found that on average, people's neuropathy symptoms improved steadily while taking ALA. Studies in the United States, including one at the Mayo Clinic, have had similar results.

IF YOU TRY IT: Some of the best studies have used injected ALA, but there's evidence that pills can help control neuropathy, too, with suggested doses ranging from 100 to 600 mg. Aside from rare allergic reactions such as skin rashes, few serious safety issues have cropped up with ALA in 30 years of testing and clinical use for neuropathy in Germany. However, it's been shown to be toxic in animals with a thiamin deficiency, so it may be worth taking ALA in conjunction with a thiamin supplement or multivitamin.

MAGNETS: A POSITIVE FORCE?

The idea of easing nerve symptoms by putting magnets in your shoes or lying on a magnetic mattress may strike you as wacky, but is it? After all, magnetic fields factor into plenty of processes in the body, from cell division to transmitting signals through the nervous system. In fact, a century ago, magnets were a popular form of medicine and were often used to treat pain. Today, such ideas are far from mainstream, but they may be worth a second look.

One of the most intriguing studies on magnet therapy involved people with chronic neuropathic foot pain. In the study (conducted by a skeptical New York neurologist), when 19 people wore magnetic insoles in their shoes for four months, 75 percent of them reported feeling significant relief. In a recent follow-up study with a much larger group of 375 people, the researcher repeated the experiment. The result: Magnets improved a wide range of symptoms, including burning, tingling, numbness, and pain. The researchers concluded that magnets affect the firing of pain receptors in the skin. It's also been suggested that magnets draw blood into areas that need more oxygen by attracting the iron in it and help blood vessel walls relax by influencing the flow of ions.

IF YOU TRY THEM: The benefits of magnets are still far from proven, but using them appears to be harmless—with a few caveats. For example, don't use magnets if you have a pacemaker, and avoid using strong magnets on your head or in the area of cancer tumors or infections. There are no standards for how strong magnets should be to treat neuropathy, but products such as magnetic insoles are widely available. Look for therapeutic magnets at a health supply store or search online under "magnetic health products."

cess

(suc•cess) *noun*

1. A favorable outcome or result.

2. The attainment of wealth, favor, or fame.

3. Better diabetes control. The logs in this chapter will help you track your success on the 10 Percent Plan, and the recipes will make it delicious.

PART FOUR

Resources

tools and recipes for
success

In this book you've discovered how making gradual changes to your daily routine can trigger a seismic shift toward better diabetes control. To help ensure your success, we've provided the following resources.

Use these logs to monitor your progress on the 10 Percent Plan and these recipes to facilitate your menu planning.

Tracking your efforts is important. Don't rely on your general impressions of what you eat and how much you exercise—write it down. Seeing the truth in black and white will reveal pitfalls and inspire you to build on your efforts. And watching your weight and blood sugar numbers go down will make it all worthwhile.

To make sure they do go down, you'll probably want to follow some of the Plate Approach menu suggestions in Step Three. To help you, we've provided recipes for some of those dishes—and many others as well—here. Remember, any food is allowed, but portion control is always key.

Personal Contract

Keep this contract as a reminder of your commitment.

Agreement with Myself

I vow that over the next six months, I will learn and implement the six steps to better diabetes control presented in the 10 Percent Plan.

My goals

Intermediate weight-loss goal: _____

Ultimate target weight: _____

My strategies

To reach these goals, I agree to:

1. Eat breakfast and small snacks so I never let myself get too hungry.
2. Follow the Plate Approach at every meal.
3. Limit my food portions.
4. Master the following disaster foods by modifying recipes and/or eating smaller portions.

   _____

   _____

   _____

5. Build up to 45 minutes of walking most days of the week.
6. Practice one stress-relief approach every day.

To track my progress, I agree to monitor and record my blood sugar regularly.

My reminders

Why I want to do all I can to control my diabetes:

1. _____

2. _____

3. _____

Signed: _____

Date: _____

Food Diary

Photocopy this form seven times, or duplicate the columns in a notebook. For one week, carry the log with you wherever you go and write down everything you eat or drink, making note of the time, portion size (use the guide on page 85 to help you estimate), and any relevant notes, such as the circumstances or what you were feeling at the time. Use nutrition labels to find the calorie content of packaged foods. To estimate calories for fresh foods, refer to a calorie-counter book or log onto www.caloriecontrol.org.

TIME	WHAT I ATE	PORTION	NOTES	CALORIES

Activity Log

Every time you do something active, note it on this form. That includes going for your daily walk and doing Sugar-Buster exercises, 30-Second Fitness Boosters, or the Day's-End Wind-Down. Also include activities such as yard work. Record the minutes spent, and add up the number at the end of the day.

	TIME	ACTIVITY	MINUTES
MONDAY			
		MONDAY TOTAL	
TUESDAY			
		TUESDAY TOTAL	
WEDNESDAY			
		WEDNESDAY TOTAL	
THURSDAY			
		THURSDAY TOTAL	
FRIDAY			
		FRIDAY TOTAL	
SATURDAY			
		SATURDAY TOTAL	
SUNDAY			
		SUNDAY TOTAL	
		WEEKLY TOTAL	

Results Tracker

Use this form to keep track of how well you're doing on the 10 Percent Plan. Start each day by writing down your morning weight. Then, at the end of the day, consider all the elements of the plan. Did you: Have breakfast and eat regularly throughout the day? Eat plenty of vegetables and limit high-calorie foods? Eat reasonable portions? Get some exercise? Manage stress well?

After reviewing your performance in each area, give yourself an overall letter grade (A, B, C, D, or F) for the day. Write a brief explanation of why you gave yourself that grade. As days go by, compare your grades with your weight patterns and use your notes to find areas where you can improve.

DATE	WEIGHT	GRADE	REASON FOR MY GRADE

Blood Sugar Log

Ask your doctor how often you should check your blood sugar, based on your personal health situation. Use your own blood sugar log, or copy this form and fill in the appropriate columns. Be sure to save the readings in a file folder: You'll want to look back on them to see how much you improve on the 10 Percent Plan.

DATE	DAY	BREAKFAST	LUNCH	DINNER	BEDTIME
	MONDAY				
	TUESDAY				
	WEDNESDAY				
	THURSDAY				
	FRIDAY				
	SATURDAY				
	SUNDAY				
	MONDAY				
	TUESDAY				
	WEDNESDAY				
	THURSDAY				
	FRIDAY				
	SATURDAY				
	SUNDAY				
	MONDAY				
	TUESDAY				
	WEDNESDAY				
	THURSDAY				
	FRIDAY				
	SATURDAY				
	SUNDAY				
	MONDAY				
	TUESDAY				
	WEDNESDAY				
	THURSDAY				
	FRIDAY				
	SATURDAY				
	SUNDAY				

Healthy Recipes

Flank Steak Roll with Spinach, Carrots and Red Pepper

SERVES 6

½ cup red wine

⅓ cup reduced-sodium soy sauce

2 tablespoons sugar

1 teaspoon garlic powder

700 g (1½ lb) flank steak, butterflied

170 g (6 oz) fresh baby spinach leaves

4 scallions, coarsely chopped

⅛ teaspoon salt

2½ cups grated peeled carrots (about 500 g/1 lb)

1 jar (1½ cups) roasted red peppers, drained

1. Combine the wine, soy sauce, sugar, and garlic powder in a large zip-close plastic bag or other container. Add the steak and turn to coat. Refrigerate for at least 2 hours or up to 4 hours.

2. Meanwhile, rinse the spinach, leaving some water clinging to the leaves. Cook, stirring frequently, in a large saucepan over medium heat just until wilted, about 1 minute. Transfer to a plate to cool.

3. Preheat the oven to 190°C (375°F). Remove the meat from the marinade and pat dry. Set the marinade aside. Spread the spinach in an even layer over the steak. Top with the scallions and sprinkle with the salt. Layer the carrots on top, then the peppers. Starting at one long side of the steak, roll tightly to enclose the filling. Secure the seam in several places with toothpicks. Place the roll, seam side down, in a shallow baking pan and brush the top with marinade.

4. Roast for 15 minutes, then spoon any pan juices on top of the meat. Roast for 20 minutes longer for medium-rare, or until desired doneness. Let stand for 10 minutes.

5. Meanwhile, boil the remaining marinade in a small saucepan just until thick enough to coat a spoon. Strain and set aside.

6. Cut the meat diagonally into 6-mm (¼-in.)-thick slices. Drizzle a little marinade on each plate and top with steak slices.

NUTRITIONAL INFORMATION

PER SERVING: 230 calories, 21 g protein, 15 g carbohydrates, 9 g fat, 4 g saturated fat, 48 mg cholesterol, 2 g fiber, 738 mg sodium

Cider-Braised Ham with Yams and Apples

SERVES 4

- 1 tablespoon Dijon mustard
- 1 tablespoon finely chopped peeled fresh ginger
- ½ teaspoon ground cloves
- 1 cup plus 1 tablespoon apple cider
- 1 yam or sweet potato, peeled and cut into 3-mm (⅛-in.)-thick slices
- 500 g (1 lb) lean ham steak
- 1 Granny Smith apple, peeled, cored, and cut into 12 wedges
- 1 tablespoon cornstarch
- ½ cup diagonally sliced green parts of scallions

1. Stir together the mustard, ginger, cloves and 1 cup of the cider in a large skillet. Bring to a simmer and add the yam. Cover tightly and simmer until partially tender, 15 minutes.

2. Add the ham steak and cover with the yam slices. Arrange the apple wedges on top. Cover and simmer until the apple and yam are tender and the ham is heated through, 10 to 15 minutes.

3. Meanwhile, stir together the cornstarch and the remaining 1 tablespoon of cider in a small bowl until well blended.

4. With a slotted spoon, transfer the ham, yam, and apple to a platter. Cover with foil to keep warm.

5. Stir a little of the hot pan juices into the cornstarch mixture until smooth. Add to the skillet and cook, stirring, over medium heat until slightly thickened, about 1 minute.

6. Divide the ham, yam, and apples among 4 plates. Spoon the skillet sauce on top and garnish with the scallions.

NUTRITIONAL INFORMATION

PER SERVING: 210 calories, 18 g protein, 25 g carbohydrates, 4 g fat, 1 g saturated fat, 38 mg cholesterol, 2 g fiber, 1,188 mg sodium

Pork Tenderloin with Honey-Mustard Sauce

SERVES 4

- 1 tablespoon chopped fresh rosemary or 1 teaspoon dried
- 2 cloves garlic, minced
- 1 teaspoon grated lemon zest
- ½ teaspoon salt
- 1 pork tenderloin (about 500 g/1 lb), trimmed of all visible fat
- ⅓ cup fresh lemon juice
- ¼ cup honey
- 3 tablespoons coarse-grain Dijon mustard
- ½ cup fat-free half-and-half
- 1 tablespoon all-purpose flour

1. Preheat the oven to 200°C (400°F). Line a small roasting pan with foil.

2. Stir together the rosemary, garlic, lemon zest, and salt in a small bowl. Rub evenly over the pork, then place the pork in the pan.

3. Stir together the lemon juice, honey, and mustard in a small bowl. Transfer half of the sauce to a small saucepan and set aside.

4. Brush the pork with 2 tablespoons of the sauce. Roast, basting 2 or 3 times with sauce, until glazed and golden brown or a thermometer inserted in the thickest portion registers 70°C (160°F), about 25 minutes.

5. Meanwhile, pour the half-and-half into a small bowl and whisk in the flour until smooth. Warm the reserved sauce over low heat. Gradually whisk in the half-and-half mixture and cook, whisking constantly, until thick, about 3 minutes. Serve with the pork.

NUTRITIONAL INFORMATION

PER SERVING: 245 calories, 25 g protein , 25 g carbohydrates, 5 g fat, 1 g saturated fat, 74 mg cholesterol, 1 g fiber, 525 mg sodium

Garden Beef Stir-Fry with Hoisin Sauce

SERVES 4

340 g (12 oz) lean sirloin
steak

2 tablespoons low-
sodium teriyaki sauce

10 medium shiitake
mushrooms

230 g (8 oz) sugar snap
peas or snow peas

2 large red bell peppers

3 tablespoons hoisin
sauce

2 tablespoons cornstarch

1¼ cups low-sodium
chicken broth or water

1 tablespoon vegetable
oil

4 scallions, thinly sliced
on the diagonal

2 cloves garlic, crushed

1. If desired, chill the steak in the freezer for 20 minutes for easier slicing. Cut across the grain into strips about 3 mm (⅛ in.) thick, then halve extra-long pieces crosswise. Toss with the teriyaki sauce in a medium bowl. Cover and refrigerate for at least 15 minutes or up to several hours.

2. Meanwhile, remove and discard the stems from the mushrooms and thinly slice the caps. Trim the ends from the peas and remove the strings. Cut the peppers into thin strips. Stir together the hoisin sauce, cornstarch, and ¼ cup of the broth in a small bowl until smooth. Set aside.

3. Heat 1 teaspoon of the oil in a large nonstick skillet or wok over high heat until hot but not smoking. Add the scallions and stir-fry for 1 minute. Transfer to a large bowl. Add the steak and garlic to the skillet and stir-fry until the meat is no longer pink, about 2 minutes. Transfer to the bowl. Add another 1 teaspoon of the oil and the mushrooms to the skillet. Stir-fry until they begin to soften, about 3 minutes, then transfer to the bowl. Add the remaining 1 teaspoon of oil and the peas and peppers. Stir-fry just until they begin to soften, 1 to 2 minutes.

4. Return the meat and vegetables to the skillet and stir in the remaining 1 cup of broth. Cover and cook over medium heat until the ingredients are heated through and the vegetables are crisp-tender, 2 to 3 minutes. Whisk the hoisin sauce mixture and add to the skillet. Stir-fry until the sauce boils, then cook for 1 minute longer.

NUTRITIONAL INFORMATION

PER SERVING: 265 calories,
21 g protein, 27 g carbohydrates, 9 g fat, 2 g saturated
fat, 48 mg cholesterol,
5 g fiber, 543 mg sodium

Hickory-Smoked Barbecued Chicken

SERVES 6

1½ teaspoons olive oil

1 medium onion, chopped

2 cloves garlic, crushed

1 can (540 ml) tomatoes in puree

⅓ cup pineapple juice

¼ cup water

2 tablespoons brown sugar

2 tablespoons light soy sauce

1 tablespoon coarse-grain Dijon mustard

1 teaspoon dried thyme

½ teaspoon salt

¼ teaspoon hickory-flavored liquid smoke

680 g (1½ lb) bone-in chicken breast halves, skin removed

680 g (1½ lb) bone-in drumsticks and thighs, skin removed

1. Coat a grill rack generously with vegetable oil. Preheat the grill.

2. Heat the oil in a medium saucepan over medium-high heat. Sauté the onion and garlic until softened, about 5 minutes. Stir in the tomatoes, pineapple juice, water, brown sugar, soy sauce, mustard, thyme, salt, and liquid smoke. Reduce the heat to medium, cover, and simmer for 5 minutes.

3. Transfer the sauce to a food processor or blender and puree. Return to the saucepan and simmer, whisking frequently, until slightly thickened, about 5 minutes. Set aside half of the sauce.

4. Brush the chicken on both sides with sauce. Grill over medium heat for 15 minutes, basting with sauce and turning the chicken halfway through cooking. Continue grilling, without basting, until no longer pink and the juices run clear, about 15 minutes. Reheat the reserved sauce to serve with the chicken.

NUTRITIONAL INFORMATION

PER SERVING: 250 calories, 31 g protein, 13 g carbohydrates, 8 g fat, 2 g saturated fat, 91 mg cholesterol, 2 g fiber, 755 mg sodium

Chicken Marsala with Herbs

SERVES 4

4 boneless skinless chicken breasts (110–170 g/ 4–6 oz each)

1 medium onion, chopped

1 teaspoon chopped garlic

¾ cup Marsala wine

4 cups tomatoes, fresh or canned

¼ teaspoon fresh-ground black pepper

2 tablespoons chopped parsley

1 tablespoon chopped fresh basil or 1 teaspoon dried

2–3 tablespoons Parmesan cheese (optional)

1. Spray a large skillet with cooking spray. Add the chicken and cook over medium heat, turning to brown on all sides. Add the onion and garlic and cook until lightly browned. Increase the heat to high, add the wine, and cook until completely reduced. Remove the chicken.

2. Reduce the heat to medium and add the tomatoes, pepper, parsley, and basil. Simmer, stirring occasionally, until the sauce begins to thicken, about 30 minutes. Return the chicken to the skillet and cook until heated through.

3. Sprinkle with the cheese, if desired.

Note: Serve over noodles if desired. Other vegetables may be added for variety, such as mushrooms, zucchini, green pepper, and broccoli.

NUTRITIONAL INFORMATION

PER SERVING: 240 calories, 29 g protein, 15 g carbohydrates, 2 g fat, 1 g saturated fat, 65 mg cholesterol, 3 g fiber, 465 mg sodium

Greek Chicken with Capers

SERVES 4

4 boneless skinless chicken breasts (110 g/ 4 oz each)

2 tablespoons all-purpose flour

2 tablespoons seasoned dried bread crumbs

1 teaspoon dried oregano

1 tablespoon olive oil

1 cup thinly sliced onion

3 cloves garlic, minced

1 cup fat-free chicken broth

½ cup white wine (optional)

2 tablespoons lemon juice

2 tablespoons capers

¼ cup crumbled feta cheese

4 black olives, chopped (optional)

1. Pound the chicken to an even thickness between 2 sheets of wax paper. Combine the flour, bread crumbs, and oregano in a shallow bowl or plate, then dredge the chicken in the mixture.

2. Heat the oil in a large nonstick skillet over medium heat. Add the chicken and brown on both sides, then remove from the skillet. Add the onion and garlic and sauté for 2 minutes. Stir in the broth, wine, and lemon juice and bring to a boil. Return the chicken to the skillet, reduce the heat, and simmer until no longer pink and the juices run clear, about 10 minutes. Sprinkle with the capers and cheese, cover, and heat gently till the cheese melts. Top with the olives, if desired.

NUTRITIONAL INFORMATION

PER SERVING: 255 calories, 30 g protein, 10 g carbohydrates, 10 g fat, 3 g saturated fat, 72 mg cholesterol, 2 g fiber, 625 mg sodium

Tex-Mex Turkey Casserole

SERVES 6

- 1 tablespoon vegetable oil
- 1 onion, coarsely chopped
- 1 tablespoon chili powder
- ½ teaspoon ground cinnamon
- ¼ teaspoon salt
- 3 tablespoons all-purpose flour
- 1 can (540 ml) diced tomatoes with mild green chiles
- 1 can (284 ml) reduced-sodium fat-free chicken broth
- 250 g (½ lb) piece deli oven-roasted turkey, sliced 2 cm (½ in.) thick and cut into cubes
- 2 zucchini, cut into 2-cm (½-in.) cubes
- 1 cup frozen corn kernels
- 1½ cups cooked long-grain white rice
- 110 g (4 oz) reduced-fat Monterey Jack cheese, shredded

1. Preheat the oven to 180°C (350°F).

2. Heat the oil in a large saucepan over medium heat. Add the onion and sauté until softened, about 5 minutes. Stir in the chili powder, cinnamon, salt, and flour. Cook, stirring, for 2 minutes. Stir in the tomatoes and broth and cook, stirring, until slightly thickened, about 2 minutes.

3. Remove from the heat and stir in the turkey, zucchini, corn, and rice. Pour into an ungreased 23 x 23 x 5-cm (9 x 9 x 2-in.) baking dish. (Recipe can be prepared ahead to this point.) Bake until bubbly, about 40 minutes. Sprinkle with the cheese and bake until melted, about 5 minutes. Let stand for 5 minutes.

NUTRITIONAL INFORMATION

PER SERVING: 265 calories, 20 g protein, 29 g carbohydrates, 8 g fat, 3 g saturated fat, 47 mg cholesterol, 3 g fiber, 831 mg sodium

Shrimp and Vegetable Stir-Fry

SERVES 4

⅔ **cup water**

⅓ **cup light soy sauce**

3 **tablespoons white wine or orange juice**

2 **tablespoons cornstarch**

1½ **teaspoons grated peeled fresh ginger**

1 **tablespoon vegetable oil**

2 **cloves garlic, minced**

500 **g (1 lb) large shrimp, peeled and deveined**

4 **cups fresh broccoli florets**

1 **large red bell pepper, cut into strips**

1 **large yellow bell pepper, cut into strips**

110 **g (4 oz) snow peas**

½ **cup drained whole baby corn**

½ **cup sliced water chestnuts**

4 **scallions, cut diagonally into 5-cm (2-in.) pieces**

1. Stir together the water, soy sauce, wine, cornstarch, and ginger in a small bowl until smooth. Set aside.

2. Heat the oil in a large wok or large, deep skillet over medium-high heat until hot. Add the garlic and stir-fry until softened, about 2 minutes. Add the shrimp and stir-fry until pink, about 3 minutes, then remove with a slotted spoon. Add the broccoli and stir-fry until bright green, about 2 minutes. Add the peppers and peas and stir-fry until crisp-tender, about 1 minute.

3. Return the shrimp to the wok. Add the corn, water chestnuts, and scallions. Pour in the reserved sauce and stir-fry until the sauce thickens and boils, about 1 minute.

NUTRITIONAL INFORMATION

PER SERVING: 265 calories, 29 g protein, 23 g carbohydrates, 6 g fat, 1 g saturated fat, 172 mg cholesterol, 4 g fiber, 992 mg sodium

Crab and Artichoke Rice Skillet

SERVES 6

- 1 tablespoon olive oil
- 3 cloves garlic, minced
- ½ medium green bell pepper, chopped
- 1 medium onion, chopped
- 2 tablespoons chopped parsley
- 1½ cups spaghetti sauce or tomato sauce
- 1 can (398 ml) artichokes, drained, liquid reserved, and quartered
- ½ can small black olives (about 30), drained and liquid reserved
- 1 package (225 g/8 oz) imitation lump crab-meat
- 4 cups cooked brown or white rice

1. Heat the oil in a large skillet. Add the garlic, pepper, and onion and sauté until softened.

2. Add the parsley, spaghetti sauce, artichokes (with liquid), olives (with liquid), and crab.

3. Cook over medium heat until hot. Stir in the rice.

NUTRITIONAL INFORMATION

PER SERVING: 285 calories, 10 g protein, 53 g carbohydrates, 6 g fat, 1 g saturated fat, 5 mg cholesterol, 9 g fiber, 625 mg sodium

Baked Cod Casserole

SERVES 4

- 500 g (1 lb) red potatoes, cut into 2-cm (½-in.)-thick slices
- 1 onion, thinly sliced
- 1 tablespoon olive oil
- ½ teaspoon salt
- 4 plum tomatoes, seeded and coarsely chopped
- 3 cloves garlic, minced
- ½ teaspoon dried oregano, crumbled
- 1½ cups arugula leaves
- 500 g (1 lb) cod, scrod, halibut, or other thick, firm-fleshed white fish, cut into 5-cm (2-in.) chunks

1. Preheat the oven to 180°C (350°F).

2. Combine the potatoes, onion, oil, and ¼ teaspoon of the salt in a 30 x 20 x 5-cm (13 x 9 x 2-in.) baking dish. Bake for 20 minutes, stirring once.

3. Stir in the tomatoes, garlic, and oregano. Spread the arugula in an even layer on top. Top with the fish and sprinkle with the remaining ¼ teaspoon of salt. Cover with foil and bake just until cooked through, 15 to 18 minutes. Transfer to plates and spoon the pan juices over each serving.

NUTRITIONAL INFORMATION

PER SERVING: 210 calories, 22 g protein, 21 g carbohydrates, 5 g fat, 1 g saturated fat, 43 mg cholesterol, 4 g fiber, 363 mg sodium

Waldorf Salad

SERVES 4

- 1 cup chopped Granny Smith or other sweet tart apples
- 1 tablespoon lemon juice
- 2 tablespoons low-fat mayonnaise
- 2 tablespoons fat-free plain yogurt
- 1 celery stalk, chopped
- ¼ cup red seedless grapes
- 2 tablespoons chopped walnuts

1. Sprinkle the apples with the lemon juice. Stir together the mayonnaise and yogurt in a small bowl.

2. Stir together the apples, celery, grapes, and walnuts in a medium bowl. Add the dressing and toss to coat.

NUTRITIONAL INFORMATION
PER SERVING: 95 calories, 2 g protein, 10 g carbohydrates, 3 g fat, 0 g saturated fat, 0 mg cholesterol, 2 g fiber, 70 mg sodium

Southwestern Black Bean Salad

SERVES 10

- 2 cans (540 ml each) black beans, drained and rinsed
- 1 can (540 ml) whole-kernel corn, drained
- 2 teaspoons minced garlic
- 1 medium green or red bell pepper, chopped
- ½ cup minced onion
- ½ cup lime juice
- 2 teaspoons dried cumin
- 2 teaspoons dried oregano
- 2 tablespoons chopped parsley
- 1 teaspoon crushed red pepper (optional)
- ½ cup cooked barley (optional)

1. Stir together the beans, corn, garlic, bell pepper, onion, lime juice, cumin, oregano, parsley, red pepper, if desired, and barley, if desired, in a large bowl.

2. Mix well and serve chilled or heated.

NUTRITIONAL INFORMATION
PER SERVING: 120 calories, 7 g protein, 23 g carbohydrates, 0 g fat, 0 g saturated fat, 0 mg cholesterol, 7 g fiber, 135 mg sodium

Tuna Salad Provençale

SERVES 4

55 g fresh green beans

225 g mixed salad greens

1 tablespoon chopped parsley

1 tablespoon snipped fresh chives

1 small red onion, thinly sliced

2 cloves garlic, chopped

2 tablespoons extra-virgin olive oil

1 tablespoon red-wine vinegar

Juice of ½ lemon

Salt and fresh-ground black pepper, to taste

1 can (540 ml) cannellini beans, drained and rinsed

12 radishes, thinly sliced

1 can (170 g) water-packed tuna, drained

7 cherry tomatoes

1 red bell pepper, seeded and thinly sliced

1 yellow bell pepper, seeded and thinly sliced

1 green bell pepper, seeded and thinly sliced

8 black olives

Fresh basil leaves

1. Place a steamer basket in a large saucepan with about 8 cm (3 in.) of water and bring to a boil over high heat. Add the green beans and steam until tender.

2. Toss the salad greens with the parsley, chives, and onion in a large bowl.

3. Stir together the garlic, oil, vinegar, and lemon juice in a small bowl. Season with the salt and pepper. Pour two-thirds of the dressing over the greens and toss to coat.

4. Arrange the green beans, cannellini beans, radishes, tuna, tomatoes, peppers, and olives on top of the greens. Add the remaining dressing and garnish with the basil.

NUTRITIONAL INFORMATION

PER SERVING: 300 calories, 24 g protein, 31 g carbohydrates, 10 g fat, 1 g saturated fat, 24 mg cholesterol, 10 g fiber, 235 mg sodium

Couscous-Stuffed Peppers

SERVES 6

- 6 **large bell peppers (any color)**
- 1 **tablespoon vegetable oil**
- 1 **small zucchini, finely chopped**
- 2 **cloves garlic, minced**
- 1 **tablespoon fresh lemon juice**
- 2 **cups cooked couscous**
- 1 **can (540 ml) chickpeas, drained and rinsed**
- 1 **ripe tomato, seeded and finely chopped**
- 1 **teaspoon dried oregano, crumbled**
- ½ **teaspoon salt**
- ¼ **teaspoon fresh-ground black pepper**
- ½ **cup crumbled feta cheese**

1. Slice the tops off the peppers to make lids. Scoop out the membranes and seeds and discard. Simmer the peppers and lids, covered, in a large saucepan of lightly salted boiling water for 5 minutes. Drain.

2. Preheat the oven to 180°C (350°F). Heat the oil in a medium saucepan over medium heat. Add the zucchini and garlic and sauté for 2 minutes. Stir in the lemon juice. Cook for 1 minute and remove from the heat. Stir in the couscous, chickpeas, tomato, oregano, salt, and pepper. Stir in the cheese.

3. Fill each pepper with the couscous mixture and place upright in a shallow baking dish. Cover with the pepper tops and bake just until the filling is heated through, about 20 minutes.

NUTRITIONAL INFORMATION

PER SERVING: 205 calories, 8 g protein, 36 g carbohydrates, 4 g fat, 1 g saturated fat, 3 mg cholesterol, 7 g fiber, 307 mg sodium

Penne with Fresh Tomato Sauce and Grilled Eggplant

SERVES 4

- 1 eggplant (500 g/1 lb), cut lengthwise into 2-cm (¾-in.)-thick slices
- ½ teaspoon salt
- 2 tablespoons olive oil
- 4 cloves garlic, thinly sliced
- 750 g (1½ lb) ripe plum tomatoes, halved, seeded, and coarsely chopped
- 1 teaspoon chopped fresh oregano or ½ teaspoon dried, crumbled
- 2 teaspoons balsamic vinegar
- ½ teaspoon sugar
- 225 g (8 oz) penne pasta
- ¼ cup shaved or shredded Parmesan cheese

1. Sprinkle the eggplant with ¼ teaspoon of the salt. Let stand for at least 30 minutes to draw out liquid.

2. Meanwhile, heat the oil in a large nonstick skillet over medium-low heat. Add the garlic and cook, stirring, for 1 minute. Add the tomatoes, oregano, and the remaining ¼ teaspoon of salt. Increase the heat to medium and cook just until the tomatoes are softened, about 6 minutes. Stir in the vinegar and sugar and cook for 30 seconds longer.

3. Preheat the grill or broiler. Rinse the eggplant and pat dry. Lightly spray both sides of the slices with cooking spray. Grill or broil 10 cm (4 in.) from the heat until softened and, if grilling, dark grill marks appear, about 5 minutes on each side. Set aside to cool slightly.

4. Meanwhile, cook the pasta according to package directions. Drain and toss with the tomato mixture. Coarsely chop the eggplant and add to the pasta, then stir in the cheese. Serve hot or at room temperature.

NUTRITIONAL INFORMATION

PER SERVING: 360 calories, 13 g protein, 59 g carbohydrates, 10 g fat, 2 g saturated fat, 4 mg cholesterol, 7 g fiber, 406 mg sodium

Rigatoni with Broccoli Rabe, Cherry Tomatoes and Roasted Garlic

SERVES 4

340 g (12 oz) rigatoni

2 small bunches broccoli rabe, tough stems removed and leaves cut crosswise into 2-cm (1-in.)-wide pieces

1 tablespoon olive oil

1 red onion, halved and thinly sliced crosswise

1 yellow bell pepper, seeded and cut length-wise into thin strips

2 scallions, thinly sliced on the diagonal

½ cup golden raisins

¼ teaspoon red pepper flakes

¼ teaspoon salt

8 cloves roasted garlic

12 cherry tomatoes, halved

Pinch of ground nutmeg

¼ teaspoon fresh-ground black pepper

¼ cup grated Parmesan cheese

1. Cook the rigatoni according to package directions. Add the broccoli rabe to the pot for the last 5 minutes of cooking. Drain.

2. Meanwhile, heat the oil in a large nonstick skillet over medium-high heat. Add the onion, bell pepper, scallions, raisins, pepper flakes, and salt. Sauté until crisp-tender, about 4 minutes. Add the garlic and sauté for 1 minute. Remove from the heat.

3. Return the pasta and broccoli rabe to the pot. Stir in the pepper mixture, tomatoes, and nutmeg. Sprinkle with the black pepper and cheese.

NUTRITIONAL INFORMATION

PER SERVING: 515 calories, 21 g protein, 98 g carbohy-drates, 7 g fat, 2 g saturated fat, 4 mg cholesterol, 6 g fiber, 506 mg sodium

Buckwheat Noodles with Tofu and Green Vegetables

SERVES 4

- 1 tablespoon vegetable oil
- 4 scallions, chopped
- 4 cloves garlic, minced
- 1 medium zucchini, halved lengthwise and cut crosswise into 0.5-cm (¼-in.)-thick slices
- ½ cup vegetable broth or reduced-sodium fat-free chicken broth
- 2 tablespoons reduced-sodium soy sauce
- 2 teaspoons cornstarch
- 1 teaspoon dark sesame oil
- 170 g (6 oz) extra-firm tofu, drained and cut into cubes
- 170 g (6 oz) buckwheat (soba) or whole wheat noodles
- 1 cup packed watercress, tough stems removed (or chopped fresh spinach)
- 2 tablespoons chopped cilantro

1. Heat the vegetable oil in a large nonstick skillet over medium-high heat. Reserve some of the dark green parts of the scallions for garnish. Add the garlic, zucchini, and the remaining scallions to the skillet. Sauté until softened, about 5 minutes.

2. Meanwhile, whisk together the broth, soy sauce, cornstarch, and sesame oil in a small bowl until smooth.

3. Add the tofu and broth mixture to the skillet. Bring to a boil and cook, stirring constantly, until the sauce thickens, 1 to 2 minutes. Remove from the heat.

4. Cook the noodles according to package directions. Drain, reserving 1 cup of the cooking liquid. Rinse under cold running water.

5. Combine the noodles, zucchini mixture, watercress, cilantro, and reserved liquid in a large bowl. Toss gently and garnish with the reserved scallions.

NUTRITIONAL INFORMATION

PER SERVING: 260 calories, 14 g protein, 40 g carbohydrates, 7 g fat, 1 g saturated fat, 0 mg cholesterol, 7 g fiber, 642 mg sodium

Zucchini and Tomato Casserole

SERVES 8

¾–1 **cup seasoned dried bread crumbs**

¼ **cup Parmesan cheese**

1–2 **teaspoons garlic powder**

Salt and fresh-ground black pepper, to taste

3–4 **medium zucchini, peeled and cut into 0.5-cm (¼-in.)-thick slices**

1 **large onion, thinly sliced**

4–5 **large tomatoes, peeled and cut into 0.5-cm (¼-in.)-thick slices**

2 **tablespoons olive oil**

1. Preheat the oven to 180°C (350°F). Spray a 2-L (2-qt) baking dish with cooking spray.

2. Stir together the bread crumbs, cheese, garlic powder, salt, and pepper in a medium bowl.

3. Place a layer of zucchini in the bottom of the baking dish. Add a layer of onion, then tomatoes. Sprinkle with a few tablespoons of the bread crumb mixture. Repeat the layers, ending with tomatoes and bread crumbs. Sprinkle with the olive oil. Cover and bake until tender, about 45 minutes.

NUTRITIONAL INFORMATION

PER SERVING: 105 calories, 4 g protein, 13 g carbohydrates, 4 g fat, 1 g saturated fat, 0 mg cholesterol, 3 g fiber, 78 mg sodium

Green Bean Casserole

SERVES 6

2 **packages frozen green beans**

1 **can (284 ml) fat-free cream of mushroom soup**

½ **cup skim or fat-free milk**

2–3 **tablespoons dehydrated minced onion**

⅓ **cup crushed French-fried onions**

1. Preheat the oven to 180°C (350°F).

2. Stir together the green beans, soup, milk, and minced onion in a 2-L (2-qt) casserole. Bake for about 30 minutes. Stir and top with the fried onions, then bake for 5 minutes longer.

NUTRITIONAL INFORMATION

PER SERVING: 90 calories, 3 g protein, 13 g carbohydrates, 3 g fat, 1 g saturated fat, 2 mg cholesterol, 16 g fiber, 360 mg sodium

Green Peas and Onions

SERVES 4

1½ cups pearl onions

1 teaspoon salt

2 cups fresh green peas

1 tablespoon light tub margarine

1 tablespoon chopped fresh rosemary

¼ teaspoon fresh-ground black pepper

1. Peel the onions. Bring 1 cup water to a boil in a large saucepan over high heat. Reduce the heat to medium, add the onions and cook, covered, for 8 minutes.

2. Shell the peas. Add to the saucepan, return to a boil, and cook, covered, for 7 to 9 minutes.

3. Meanwhile, melt the margarine in a small saucepan over low heat. Add the rosemary and cook for 2 to 3 minutes.

4. Drain the peas and onions. Add the margarine and pepper and toss gently.

NUTRITIONAL INFORMATION

PER SERVING: 106 calories, 5 g protein, 16 g carbohydrates, 5 g fat, 1 g saturated fat, 0 mg cholesterol, 5 g fiber, 70 mg sodium

Steamed Sesame Spinach

SERVES 4

500 g (1 lb) fresh spinach, stems removed

⅛ teaspoon red pepper flakes

½ teaspoon dark sesame oil

1 teaspoon fresh lemon juice

1 tablespoon sesame seeds, toasted

1 teaspoon salt

1. Place a steamer basket in a medium saucepan with 5 to 8 cm (2 to 3 in.) of water. Add the spinach and pepper flakes and steam until tender, 3 to 5 minutes.

2. Transfer to a serving bowl. Add the oil, salt, and lemon juice and toss. Sprinkle with the sesame seeds.

NUTRITIONAL INFORMATION

PER SERVING: 35 calories, 3 g protein, 4 g carbohydrates, 2 g fat, 0 g saturated fat, 0 mg cholesterol, 3 g fiber, 90 mg sodium

Grilled Vegetable Salad

SERVES 6

1 **small eggplant (340 g/¾ lb)**

1 **small bulb fennel (170 g/6 oz) trimmed**

1 **medium yellow summer squash**

1 **medium zucchini**

½ **teaspoon salt**

1 **small red bell pepper, halved lengthwise and seeded**

3 **plum tomatoes, halved lengthwise and seeded**

2 **tablespoons olive oil**

2 **cloves garlic, minced**

1 **teaspoon finely chopped fresh marjoram or ½ teaspoon dried, crumbled**

1½ **tablespoons balsamic vinegar**

1. Preheat the grill to medium-high. Cut the eggplant, fennel, squash, and zucchini lengthwise into 1.5-cm (½-in.)-thick slices. Sprinkle with ¼ teaspoon of the salt and spray generously with cooking spray.

2. Grill the pepper, skin side down, until blackened and blistered, 3 to 4 minutes. Remove from the heat.

3. Grill the eggplant, fennel, squash, and zucchini on one side until grill marks are dark brown but the vegetables are still very firm, about 4 minutes. Turn and grill the other side until browned and just tender, about 3 minutes for the squash and zucchini and 5 to 6 minutes longer for the eggplant and fennel. Remove from the heat.

4. Coat the cut sides of the tomatoes with cooking spray. Grill, cut sides down, just until light grill marks appear, about 3 minutes.

5. Heat the oil in a small skillet over medium heat. Add the garlic, marjoram, and the remaining ¼ teaspoon of salt. Sauté for 1 minute.

6. Peel the grilled pepper and cut into strips. Cut the rest of the vegetables into bite-size chunks. Transfer to a medium bowl and add the olive oil mixture and vinegar. Toss to coat and serve at room temperature.

NUTRITIONAL INFORMATION

PER SERVING: 85 calories, 2 g protein, 10 g carbohydrates, 5 g fat, 1 g saturated fat, 0 mg cholesterol, 4 g fiber, 211 mg sodium

Pineapple Coleslaw

SERVES 8

- 1 bag coleslaw mix
- 1 green bell pepper, finely chopped
- 1 can (398 ml) unsweetened crushed pineapple
- 2 tablespoons fat-free mayonnaise
- 1 tablespoon wine vinegar
- 1 teaspoon Dijon or honey mustard
- 2 packets Splenda or Equal sweetener

  Salt and fresh-ground black pepper, to taste

1. Combine the coleslaw mix, green pepper, and pineapple (with liquid) in a large bowl.

2. Stir together the mayonnaise, vinegar, mustard, sweetener, salt, and pepper in a small bowl. Add to the cabbage mixture and stir well to combine. Chill for several hours or overnight. Mix well before serving.

NUTRITIONAL INFORMATION

PER SERVING: 60 calories, 1 g protein, 12 g carbohydrates, 0 g fat, 0 g saturated fat, 0 mg cholesterol, 2 g fiber, 10 mg sodium

Roasted Carrots with Rosemary

SERVES 6

- 500 g (1 lb) large carrots, peeled and cut into 5 x 0.5-cm (2 x ¼-in.) sticks
- ¼ teaspoon salt
- 1½ teaspoons olive oil
- 1 teaspoon minced fresh rosemary or ½ teaspoon dried, crumbled

1. Preheat the oven to 200°C (400°F).

2. Mound the carrots on a baking sheet. Sprinkle with the salt and drizzle with the oil, then toss gently. Spread into a single layer.

3. Roast for 10 minutes. Stir in the rosemary and roast until crisp-tender and lightly browned in spots, 7 to 10 minutes.

NUTRITIONAL INFORMATION

PER SERVING: 45 calories, 1 g protein, 8 g carbohydrates, 1 g fat, 0 g saturated fat, 0 mg cholesterol, 2 g fiber, 136 mg sodium

German Potato Salad with Dijon Vinaigrette

750 g (1½ lb) small red
    potatoes, scrubbed
    and quartered

½ teaspoon salt

4 slices turkey bacon

1 small onion, chopped

¼ cup apple cider
    vinegar

2 tablespoons sugar

1 tablespoon coarse-
    grain Dijon mustard

1 teaspoon olive oil

½ teaspoon fresh-ground
    black pepper

¼ cup finely chopped
    sweet pickles

¼ cup finely chopped red
    bell pepper

¼ cup minced parsley

1. Place the potatoes and enough water to cover in a large saucepan. Add ¼ teaspoon of the salt and bring to a boil over high heat. Reduce the heat to medium and cook until tender, about 10 minutes. Drain and keep warm.

2. Meanwhile, cut the bacon in half crosswise and cook in a large, deep nonstick skillet until crisp. Drain on paper towels, then crumble. Sauté the onion in the pan juices until golden, about 7 minutes.

3. Shake the vinegar, sugar, mustard, oil, black pepper, and the remaining ¼ teaspoon salt in a jar, then whisk into the skillet. Bring to a simmer and cook until fragrant, about 2 minutes. Add the potatoes, pickles, red pepper, and half of the bacon. Cook, stirring, until the potatoes are evenly coated and heated through, about 2 minutes. Sprinkle with the parsley and the remaining bacon. Serve warm or at room temperature.

NUTRITIONAL INFORMATION

PER SERVING: 190 calories, 5 g protein, 36 g carbohydrates, 3 g fat, 1 g saturated fat, 7 mg cholesterol, 3 g fiber, 597 mg sodium

Scalloped Potatoes

4 onions, thinly sliced

½–¾ cup chicken broth

1 can fat-free evapo-
    rated milk

750 g (1½ lb) potatoes,
    peeled and sliced

Salt and fresh-ground
    black pepper, to taste

Pinch of paprika

1. Preheat the oven to 220°C (425°F). Lightly spray a shallow 2-L (2-qt) baking dish with cooking spray.

2. Bring the onions and ½ cup of the broth to a boil in a non-stick skillet over medium heat. Reduce the heat and simmer, stirring occasionally, until tender, about 10 minutes, adding more broth if the mixture becomes dry. Add the milk and heat for about 10 minutes.

3. Arrange half of the potatoes in the baking dish and season with the salt and pepper. Spoon half of the onion mixture on top. Add another layer of potatoes, then of onions. Lightly season with the salt and pepper and sprinkle with the paprika. Bake uncovered until lightly browned and the potatoes are tender when a fork is inserted in the middle, about 30 minutes.

NUTRITIONAL INFORMATION

PER SERVING: 135 calories, 6 g protein, 28 g carbohydrates, 0 g fat, 0 g saturated fat, 0 mg cholesterol, 3 g fiber, 106 mg sodium

Irish Mashed Potatoes with Cabbage and Leeks

SERVES 8

1 kg (2 lb) Yukon Gold potatoes, quartered

3 cans (284 ml each) reduced-sodium fat-free chicken broth

500 g (1 lb) leeks, trimmed, thinly sliced, and rinsed

1 cup 1% milk

3 cloves garlic, crushed

1 bay leaf

1 head green cabbage, cored and thinly sliced

¼ cup cold water

¼ teaspoon ground nutmeg

¼ teaspoon salt

¼ teaspoon white pepper

2 tablespoons unsalted butter

¼ cup minced chives

1. Place the potatoes, broth, and enough water to cover in a large saucepan. Bring to a boil and cook until tender, 20 to 25 minutes.

2. Meanwhile, combine the leeks, milk, garlic, and bay leaf in another large saucepan. Cover and bring to a boil. Reduce the heat and simmer until the leeks are softened, 15 to 20 minutes. Drain, reserving the leeks, milk, and garlic separately. Discard the bay leaf.

3. In the same saucepan, combine the cabbage and water. Cover and bring to a gentle boil. Cook until tender, 10 to 15 minutes, then drain. Squeeze dry and chop finely.

4. Drain the potatoes and transfer to a large bowl. Add the milk and garlic and mash. Stir in the leeks, cabbage, nutmeg, salt, pepper, and butter. Top with the chives.

NUTRITIONAL INFORMATION

PER SERVING: 165 calories, 6 g protein, 29 g carbohydrates, 4 g fat, 2 g saturated fat, 9 mg cholesterol, 3 g fiber, 379 mg sodium

Praline Sweet Potato Casserole

SERVES 12

- 4 cups cooked sweet potatoes or yams (about 1 kg/2 lb)
- ½ cup Splenda sweetener
- 4 egg whites or ½ cup liquid egg substitute
- ½ teaspoon salt
- 1 teaspoon vanilla extract
- ½ cup brown sugar or brown sugar substitute
- ¼ cup chopped pecans
- ¼ cup all-purpose flour
- 2 tablespoons light tub margarine

1. Preheat the oven to 180°C (350°F). Lightly grease (or spray with cooking spray) a shallow 2-L (2-qt) baking dish.

2. Combine the sweet potatoes, sweetener, egg whites, salt, and vanilla in a food processor or blender and process until smooth. Spoon into the baking dish.

3. Stir together the brown sugar, pecans, flour, and margarine in a medium bowl. Lightly sprinkle over the sweet potato mixture. Spray the top with butter-flavored spray and bake until lightly browned, about 30 minutes.

> **NUTRITIONAL INFORMATION**
>
> PER SERVING: 150 calories, 3 g protein, 27 g carbohydrates, 2 g fat, 0 g saturated fat, 0 mg cholesterol, 2 g fiber, 172 mg sodium

Sage Dressing

SERVES 4

- ½ cup finely chopped celery
- ½ cup chopped onions
- 1 tablespoon chopped parsley
- 1½ teaspoons sage
- 2¾ cups dry bread cubes
- 1½ cups chicken broth

1. Preheat the oven to 180°C (350°F). Spray a 2-L (2-qt) baking dish with cooking spray.

2. Spray a medium nonstick skillet with cooking spray. Add the celery and onions and cook, stirring occasionally, until tender. Stir in the parsley and sage.

2. Place the bread cubes in the baking dish and top with the onion mixture. Drizzle with 1 cup of the broth. Toss gently to combine and add the remaining ½ cup of broth if the dressing is too dry. Bake uncovered until lightly browned, about 30 minutes.

> **NUTRITIONAL INFORMATION**
>
> PER SERVING: 70 calories, 3 g protein, 13 g carbohydrates, 1 g fat, 0 g saturated fat, 0 mg cholesterol, 1 g fiber, 305 mg sodium

Nutted Lemon Barley

SERVES 8

- 2 tablespoons olive oil
- 2 onions, finely chopped
- 3 celery stalks, finely chopped
- 1 cup pearl barley, rinsed
- 2½ cups low-sodium chicken broth
- 1 teaspoon finely grated lemon zest
- ½ teaspoon dried oregano
- ⅛ teaspoon salt
- ⅛ teaspoon fresh-ground black pepper
- 2 tablespoons sunflower seeds
- 1 tablespoon fresh lemon juice
- ¼ cup golden raisins
- 2 tablespoons chopped parsley

1. Heat the oil in a large, heavy saucepan over medium heat. Add the onions and celery and sauté, stirring, until softened and lightly browned, about 7 minutes. Stir in the barley until coated with oil. Add the broth, lemon zest, oregano, salt, and pepper.

2. Bring the broth to a boil, then reduce the heat. Cover and simmer, stirring occasionally, until the barley is nearly cooked through and almost all the liquid is absorbed, about 40 minutes.

3. Meanwhile, toast the sunflower seeds in a nonstick skillet over medium heat, stirring frequently or shaking the skillet, until golden brown. Transfer to a plate.

4. Stir the lemon juice and raisins into the barley mixture. Cover, remove from the heat, and let stand for about 5 minutes. Gently stir in the sunflower seeds and parsley just until combined.

NUTRITIONAL INFORMATION

PER SERVING: 170 calories, 4 g protein, 28 g carbohydrates, 5 g fat, 1 g saturated fat, 0 mg cholesterol, 5 g fiber, 71 mg sodium

Bulgur with Spring Vegetables

SERVES 6

1¼ cups coarse-ground bulgur wheat

3 tablespoons fresh lemon juice

1 teaspoon salt

½ teaspoon fresh-ground black pepper

2 tablespoons olive oil

2 leeks, halved lengthwise, cut crosswise into 2-cm (1-in.) pieces, and well washed

2 cloves garlic, minced

12 spears asparagus, cut into 5-cm (2-in.) pieces

1 cup frozen peas

¼ cup chopped fresh mint

1. In a medium saucepan, bring 3½ cups water to a boil. Combine the bulgur and water in a large heatproof bowl. Let stand until the bulgur is tender, about 30 minutes; stir after 15 minutes. Drain in a large, fine-meshed sieve.

2. Whisk together the lemon juice, salt, pepper, and 1 tablespoon of the oil in a large bowl. Add the bulgur and fluff with a fork.

3. Heat the remaining 1 tablespoon of oil in a large skillet over medium heat. Add the leeks and garlic and cook until the leeks are tender, about 5 minutes. Transfer to the bowl.

4. Place a steamer basket in a large saucepan with about 8 cm (3 in.) of water. Add the asparagus and steam until tender, about 4 minutes. Add the peas during the final 30 seconds of steaming. Add the asparagus, peas, and mint to the bulgur and toss to combine. Serve at room temperature or chilled.

NUTRITIONAL INFORMATION

PER SERVING: 185 calories, 6 g protein, 32 g carbohydrates, 5 g fat, 1 g saturated fat, 0 mg cholesterol, 8 g fiber, 330 mg sodium

Hearty Turkey Chili

SERVES 8

250 g (½ lb) lean ground turkey

1 medium onion, chopped

1 small green bell pepper, chopped

1 tablespoon chili powder, or to taste

1 teaspoon dry mustard

1 can (540 ml) tomatoes

1 can (213 ml) tomato sauce

1 clove garlic, minced

1 can (284 ml) sliced mushrooms or ⅔ cup sliced fresh mushrooms

2 cans (398 ml each) kidney beans, drained and rinsed

1. Spray a large skillet with cooking spray. Add the turkey and cook until browned. Drain off any fat.

2. Add the onion, pepper, chili powder, and mustard and cook for 5 minutes. Add the tomatoes, tomato sauce, garlic, mushrooms, and beans.

3. Simmer for 30 to 45 minutes.

NUTRITIONAL INFORMATION
PER SERVING: 175 calories, 14 g protein, 21 g carbohydrates, 4 g fat, 2 g saturated fat, 24 mg cholesterol, 10 g fiber, 580 mg sodium

Beefy Mushroom-Barley Stew

SERVES 6

340 g (12 oz) beef round, cut into 2-cm (1-in.) cubes

3 medium onions, coarsely chopped

280 g (10 oz) mushrooms, sliced

3 large carrots, sliced

½ cup pearl barley, rinsed

7 cups reduced-sodium beef broth

1 cup dry red wine or no-salt-added tomato juice

½ teaspoon salt

½ teaspoon fresh-ground black pepper

1 cup frozen green peas

2 teaspoons fresh lemon juice

1. Spray a soup pot or large, heavy saucepan with cooking spray. Warm over medium-high heat until hot but not smoking. Add the beef and sauté until browned, about 5 minutes. With a slotted spoon, transfer to a double layer of paper towels to drain.

2. Sauté the onions and mushrooms in the pan juices until the onions are golden, about 7 minutes. Return the beef to the pot. Stir in the carrots, barley, broth, wine, salt, and pepper and bring to a boil.

3. Reduce the heat to medium-low. Simmer, partially covered, until the beef and barley are tender, about 45 minutes. Stir in the peas and cook until tender, about 5 minutes. Remove from the heat and stir in the lemon juice.

NUTRITIONAL INFORMATION

PER SERVING: 255 calories, 19 g protein, 29 g carbohydrates, 5 g fat, 1 g saturated fat, 26 mg cholesterol, 6 g fiber, 341 mg sodium

Greek Spinach, Egg and Lemon Soup

SERVES 4

3 scallions, thinly sliced

3 cloves garlic, minced

3 cups reduced-sodium fat-free chicken broth

1 package (about 300 g/10 oz) frozen chopped spinach

½ teaspoon dried oregano

1 cup cooked brown rice

1 teaspoon grated lemon zest

3 tablespoons fresh lemon juice

½ teaspoon salt

1 large egg plus 2 egg whites

1. Combine the scallions, garlic, and ¼ cup of the broth in a medium saucepan. Cook over medium heat until the scallions are tender, about 2 minutes.

2. Add the spinach, oregano, and the remaining 2¾ cups of broth and bring to a boil. Reduce the heat, cover, and simmer until the spinach is tender, about 5 minutes.

3. Stir in the rice, lemon zest, lemon juice, and salt and return to a simmer. Remove ½ cup of the liquid and whisk into the egg and egg whites in a medium bowl. Whisking constantly, add the egg mixture to the soup.

NUTRITIONAL INFORMATION

PER SERVING: 115 calories, 8 g protein, 17 g carbohydrates, 2 g fat, 1 g saturated fat, 53 mg cholesterol, 3 g fiber, 728 mg sodium

Winter Weight-Loss Soup

SERVES 14

2 cans (540 ml each) whole tomatoes

1 can (680 ml) tomato sauce

1 litre (1 qt) water

4 beef bouillon cubes

1–2 cloves garlic, chopped

1 large turnip

1 green bell pepper

½ celery stalk

1 large onion

1 small zucchini

2 large carrots

1 small head cabbage, shredded

225 g (8 oz) fresh or frozen green beans

1 cup thawed frozen chopped spinach

1 teaspoon dried thyme

1 teaspoon dried oregano

1 bay leaf

Salt and fresh-ground black pepper, to taste

1. Combine the tomatoes, tomato sauce, water, bouillon, and garlic in a large soup pot. Chop the turnip, bell pepper, celery, onion, zucchini, and carrots into large pieces and add to the pot.

2. Cook at a slow boil until the vegetables are soft but still firm, at least 1 hour. Stir in the cabbage, beans, spinach, thyme, oregano, bay leaf, salt, and pepper.

3. Simmer until cooked through but firm. Discard the bay leaf before serving.

NUTRITIONAL INFORMATION

PER SERVING: 50 calories, 3 g protein, 11 g carbohydrates, 0 g fat, 0 g saturated fat, 0 mg cholesterol, 3 g fiber, 625 mg sodium

---

Breads

Bread Machine Hearty Oatmeal Loaf

MAKES 16 SLICES

1¼ cups water

1½ teaspoons salt

3 tablespoons sugar
or ¼ cup Splenda
sweetener

2 tablespoons nonfat dry
milk

2 tablespoons oil

½ cup old-fashioned oats

2 tablespoons wheat germ

2 tablespoons flax meal
(optional)

3 tablespoons chopped
walnuts

½ cup whole wheat flour

3 cups all-purpose flour

2 teaspoons active dry
yeast

1. Add the ingredients to a bread machine according to
the manufacturer's instructions.

2. Use the white or whole wheat bread setting for a 680-g
(1½-lb) loaf.

NUTRITIONAL INFORMATION

PER SLICE: 140 calories, 5 g protein, 23 g carbohydrates, 3 g fat,
0 g saturated fat, 0 mg cholesterol, 3 g fiber, 205 mg sodium

Bran Muffins

MAKES 24 MUFFINS

1 cup bran cereal (such as
All-Bran or Fiber One)

1½ cups mashed banana or
unsweetened apple-
sauce

¼ cup skim or fat-free milk

1 cup whole wheat flour

½ cup old-fashioned oats

1 tablespoon baking
powder

½ teaspoon baking soda

1 tablespoon honey

2 tablespoons dark
molasses

1 teaspoon cinnamon

2 egg whites or 1 whole
egg or ¼ cup liquid egg
substitute

⅔ cup blueberries or ¼ cup
craisins and ¼ cup mini
chocolate chips

1. Preheat the oven to 200°C (400°F). Spray two 12-cup
muffin pans with cooking spray or insert paper liners.

2. Combine the cereal, banana, and milk in a large bowl. Let
stand for about 5 minutes.

3. Add the flour, oats, baking powder, baking soda, honey,
molasses, cinnamon, egg whites, and blueberries and stir
until combined. Spoon the batter into the pans and bake
for 20 minutes.

NUTRITIONAL INFORMATION

PER MUFFIN: 60 calories, 2 g protein, 13 g carbohydrates, 0 g fat,
0 g saturated fat, 0 mg cholesterol, 3 g fiber, 106 mg sodium

Desserts

Key Lime–Yogurt Mousse

SERVES 8

- 1 package sugar-free lime Jell-O
- 2 cups fat-free sugar-free key lime yogurt
- 1 cup fat-free whipped topping

1. In a small saucepan, bring ½ cup water to a boil. Pour into a medium bowl, add the Jell-O, and stir to dissolve.

2. Stir in the yogurt until blended, then fold in three-quarters of the topping.

3. Refrigerate for about 30 minutes and serve with the remaining topping.

NUTRITIONAL INFORMATION
PER SERVING: 90 calories, 3 g protein, 14 g carbohydrates, 0 g fat, 0 g saturated fat, 0 mg cholesterol, 0 g fiber, 43 mg sodium

Chocolate–Banana Pudding Parfait

SERVES 4

- 1 package sugar-free chocolate pudding
- 2 cups skim or fat-free milk
- 1 banana, sliced
- ½ cup fat-free or light whipped topping
- 1 teaspoon shaved chocolate

1. Make the pudding according to package directions. Layer with the banana in 4 parfait glasses.

2. Add a dollop of the topping and garnish with the chocolate.

NUTRITIONAL INFORMATION
PER SERVING: 150 calories, 5 g protein, 30 g carbohydrates, 0 g fat, 0 g saturated fat, 3 mg cholesterol, 0 g fiber, 395 mg sodium

Lemon Angel Food Cake with Strawberries

SERVES 12

2 bags (300 g each) frozen strawberries, thawed

½ cup orange juice

12 large egg whites, at room temperature

1¼ teaspoons cream of tartar

½ teaspoon salt

1¼ cups sugar

3 tablespoons grated lemon zest

1 teaspoon vanilla extract

1 cup all-purpose flour

1. Combine the strawberries and orange juice in a large bowl and refrigerate.

2. Preheat the oven to 160°C (325°F). Beat the egg whites, cream of tartar, and salt with an electric mixer in a large bowl until foamy. Gradually beat in the sugar, 2 tablespoons at a time, until thick, soft peaks form. Beat in the lemon zest and vanilla.

3. Gently fold the flour into the egg whites, ¼ cup at a time, until incorporated. Spoon into an ungreased 25 x 11-cm (10 x 4½-in.) tube pan. Bake until the top springs back when lightly pressed, about 50 minutes.

4. Invert the pan to cool. (If the pan doesn't have legs, invert it on the neck of a bottle.) Let cool completely, then remove by running a metal spatula around the edges and center and inverting onto a cake platter. Serve with the strawberries and juice.

NUTRITIONAL INFORMATION

PER SERVING: 160 calories, 5 g protein, 35 g carbohydrate, 0 g fat, 0 g saturated fat, 0 mg cholesterol, 1 g fiber, 153 mg sodium

Ambrosia Fruit Salad

SERVES 12

- 1 package sugar-free instant vanilla pudding
- 2 cups skim or fat-free milk
- 1 can (398 ml) juice-packed tropical fruit, drained
- 1 can (398 ml) juice-packed fruit cocktail, drained
- 1 can (398 ml) juice-packed pineapple tid-bits, drained
- 1 can (398 ml) juice-packed mandarin oranges, drained
- ½ cup fat-free or light whipped topping

1. Combine the pudding and the milk in a large bowl.

2. Fold in tropical fruit, fruit cocktail, pineapple, oranges, and topping. Refrigerate until ready to serve.

> **NUTRITIONAL INFORMATION**
>
> **PER SERVING:** 145 calories, 3 g protein, 35 g carbohydrates, 0 g fat, 0 g saturated fat, 0 mg cholesterol, 2 g fiber, 32 mg sodium

Peach Crisp

SERVES 9

- 4 cups sliced fresh or frozen peaches
- ¾ cup Splenda sweetener
- 1 teaspoon ground cinnamon
- ½ cup old-fashioned oats
- 2 tablespoons chopped walnuts
- ½ cup graham cracker crumbs
- ½ cup brown sugar
- 2 tablespoons light tub margarine

1. Preheat the oven to 180°C (350°F).

2. Place the peaches in a 20 x 20-cm (8 x 8-in.) baking dish and sprinkle with the sweetener and cinnamon.

3. For the topping, stir together the oats, walnuts, graham cracker crumbs, and brown sugar in a medium bowl. Blend in the margarine. Scatter the oat mixture over the peaches and bake until crisp on top, about 45 minutes.

Note: For an even quicker version of Peach Crisp, top with peaches-and-cream instant oatmeal instead of making the topping.

> **NUTRITIONAL INFORMATION**
>
> **PER SERVING:** 140 calories, 2 g protein, 27 g carbohydrates, 3 g fat, 1 g saturated fat, 0 mg cholesterol, 2 g fiber, 75 mg sodium

Pumpkin Pie

SERVES 8

Crust

- 1 cup all-purpose flour
- ½ teaspoon salt
- 6 tablespoons light stick margarine, chilled
- 2–3 tablespoons ice water

Filling

- 1 can (398 ml) pumpkin
- 1 can (385 ml) fat-free evaporated milk
- 4 egg whites
- 18 packets Equal sweetener or ¾ cup Equal Spoonful or Splenda sweetener
- ¼ teaspoon salt
- 1 teaspoon ground cinnamon
- ½ teaspoon ground ginger
- ⅓ teaspoon ground cloves

1. Preheat the oven to 220°C (425°F).

2. *To make the crust:* Stir together the flour and salt in a medium bowl. Cut in the margarine. Gradually add the water and stir until moistened. Shape into a ball and roll into a 10-inch circle. Place in a 22-cm (9-in.) pie pan and crimp the edges.

3. *To make the filling:* Beat the pumpkin, milk, and egg whites with an electric mixer in a medium bowl. Add the sweetener, salt, cinnamon, ginger, and cloves and beat until combined.

4. Pour the filling into the crust and bake for 15 minutes, then reduce the heat to 180°C (350°F) and bake for about 40 minutes longer. Cool on a wire rack.

> **NUTRITIONAL INFORMATION**
>
> **PER SERVING:** 155 calories, 7 g protein, 22 g carbohydrates, 5 g fat, 1 g saturated fat, 0 mg cholesterol, 2 g fiber, 380 mg sodium

Fruit and Cream–Filled Sponge Cakes

SERVES 8

- 2 tablespoons all-fruit preserves
- 1 cup strawberries, blueberries, raspberries, or other fruit, washed, trimmed, and sliced as necessary
- ¾ cup blended low-fat yogurt (same flavor as fruit)
- ¾ cup reduced-fat or fat-free sour cream
- 8 sponge cake cups

1. Place the preserves in a small dish and microwave for 1 minute to soften. Stir together with the fruit in a medium bowl, coating evenly.

2. Stir together the yogurt and sour cream in a small bowl. Spoon 2 to 3 tablespoons into each cake cup and top with 2 to 4 tablespoons of the fruit.

> **NUTRITIONAL INFORMATION**
>
> **PER SERVING:** 105 calories, 2 g protein, 45 g carbohydrates, 1 g fat, 0 g saturated fat, 45 mg cholesterol, 1 g fiber, 40 mg sodium

Recipe Index

General Index